Arctic Aria

Arctic Aria

Polar Wildlife Lullabies

Rafeal Mechlore

Leader Enterprises

CONTENTS

INDEX 1

INTRODUCTION 3

1 | Chapter 1 16

2 | Chapter 2 37

3 | Chapter 3 54

4 | Chapter 4 73

5 | Chapter 5 95

6 | Chapter 6 112

7 | Chapter 7 128

8 | Chapter 8 152

9 | Chapter 9 173

10 | Chapter 10 192

11 | Chapter 11 213

INDEX

Introduction

1. Brief Overview of the Arctic
2. Importance of Arctic Wildlife
3. Purpose of the Book

Chapter 1: The Icy Wonderland
1.1 Introduction to the Arctic Environment
1.2 Unique Features of the Arctic
1.3 The Polar Night and Midnight Sun
1.4 How Climate Change is Affecting the Arctic

Chapter 2: Arctic Lullabies
2.1 Introduction to Polar Wildlife Lullabies
2.2 The Role of Lullabies in Nature
2.3 Understanding Arctic Animal Behavior
2.4 The Connection Between Animal Sounds and Lullabies

Chapter 3: The Walrus's Whisper
3.1 Introduction to the Walrus
3.2 The Sounds of Walrus
3.3 The Walrus's Importance in the Arctic Ecosystem
3.4 A Walrus-inspired Lullaby

Chapter 4: The Beluga's Ballad
4.1 Introduction to the Beluga Whale
4.2 The Melodic Calls of Belugas
4.3 The Life of Beluga Whales in the Arctic
4.4 A Beluga-inspired Lullaby

Chapter 5: The Polar Bear's Hush
5.1 Introduction to the Polar Bear
5.2 The Silent World of Polar Bears
5.3 The Role of Polar Bears in the Arctic Food Chain
5.4 A Polar Bear-inspired Lullaby

Chapter 6: The Arctic Fox's Serenade
6.1 Introduction to the Arctic Fox
6.2 The Mysterious Calls of Arctic Foxes
6.3 The Adaptations of Arctic Foxes
6.4 An Arctic Fox-inspired Lullaby

Chapter 7: The Seal's Slumber Song
7.1 Introduction to Arctic Seals
7.2 The Haunting Songs of Seals
7.3 The Diversity of Seal Species in the Arctic
7.4 A Seal-inspired Lullaby

Chapter 8: The Arctic Owl's Sonata
8.1 Introduction to Arctic Owls
8.2 The Enchanting Hoots of Arctic Owls
8.3 The Survival Strategies of Arctic Owls
8.4 An Arctic Owl-inspired Lullaby

Chapter 9: The Narwhal's Whistle
9.1 Introduction to the Narwhal
9.2 The Mystical Whistles of Narwhals
9.3 The Fascinating Tusk of Narwhals
9.4 A Narwhal-inspired Lullaby

Chapter 10: The Svalbard Siren's Aria
10.1 Introduction to Svalbard
10.2 The Unique Wildlife of Svalbard
10.3 Conservation Efforts in the Arctic
10.4 A Svalbard-inspired Lullaby

Chapter 11: Composing Arctic Lullabies
11.1 The Creative Process
11.2 Collaborating with Arctic Researchers
11.3 Recording and Sharing the Lullabies
11.4 The Impact of Arctic Aria on Conservation

INTRODUCTION

In the most distant ranges of our planet, where the frigid hold of winter is felt all year, a surprising ensemble of life works out underneath the moving Aurora Borealis. The Cold, an immense and apparently forsaken breadth, is home to an abundance of interesting and diligent animals. In this immaculate, frozen wild, a remarkable show of sounds fills the fresh polar air, reverberating across the tundra, ice, and freezing waters. The cradlesongs of the Icy, nonetheless, are not sung by people. All things considered, they are murmured, whistled, hooted, and, surprisingly, thundered by the wonderful untamed life that call this outrageous climate home.

"Icy Aria: Polar Untamed life Bedtime songs" is an excursion into the core of the Cold, where the dazzling biodiversity of the normal world joins with the charming force of music. This book welcomes you to investigate the frosty wonderland, acquainting you with the charming occupants of the area while diving into their remarkable vocalizations. Through these parts, we will wind around an account of the Icy's one of a kind bedtime songs, uncovering how these sounds have molded and keep on forming the rhythms of life in perhaps of Earth's most delicate environment.

The Icy, portrayed by its super cool, long polar evenings, and apparently vast territories of ice and snow, may seem aloof from the get go. Nonetheless, exactly these brutal circumstances have led to a large number of inconceivable variations and unpredictable connections among its occupants. From the appealling polar bear to the slippery Icy fox, from the great beluga whale to the legendary narwhal, every species has developed to flourish in this requesting climate.

However, past the methods for surviving and stunning scenes, there is a more profound layer to the Cold's charm - a layer that addresses the interconnectedness of all life on The planet. This secret layer comprises of the eerie, mitigating, and some of the time thrilling sounds created by the creatures of the Cold, which assume fundamental parts in their day to day routines, from correspondence and route to drawing in mates and supporting their young.

The idea of bedtime songs is general among human societies, where alleviating tunes and delicate rhythms are utilized to slip infants into sleep. In the Icy, nonetheless, this idea stretches out past human culture. The actual creatures make and use bedtime songs, each with its interesting reason and importance. The walrus murmurs in obscurity, the beluga whale sings to the profundities of the sea, the polar bear tracks down solace peacefully, and the Icy fox serenades the Icy evening.

The seal's sleep tune conveys across the cold waves, the Icy owl's sonata fills the freezing air, and the narwhal's whistle enters the frosty ocean. Every one of these tunes, these Cold cradlesongs, is a demonstration of the perplexing trap of life that exists in this remote corner of the world.

"Icy Aria" is a festival of this ensemble of sound, an excursion into the core of the Cold where you can pay attention to the dazzling tunes of polar untamed life and become submerged in the magnificence of this remarkable melodic scene. It is an investigation of how these children's songs are entwined with the everyday battles and wins of Cold creatures, revealing insight into the exceptional transformations and ways of behaving that have advanced in light of the Icy's difficulties.

While the Cold's music spellbinds us, it likewise fills in as a distinct sign of the delicate idea of this biological system. The Cold, as one of the World's most weak locales to environmental change, faces quick and significant adjustments because of increasing temperatures and moving ice designs. These progressions influence the creatures' lifestyle as well as have repercussions for the whole planet. Accordingly, the Cold's bedtime songs take on an earnest importance as they highlight the requirement for preservation and insurance.

All through the pages of "Cold Aria," you will set out on an excursion into the profundities of the Icy wild. You won't just experience the charming animals that call this district home yet in addition gain a profound comprehension of their vocal articulations and the essential jobs these sounds play in their reality. As we venture further into this captivating world, you will find how we, as people, have been roused by the Icy's normal sounds to make an assortment of children's songs that give proper respect to this wondrous spot.

The force of music is significant and rises above limits, uniting individuals and motivating activity. Through "Cold Aria," we will investigate how the language of music can overcome any issues between the Icy wild and the remainder of the world, cultivating a feeling of association and obligation toward the protection of this indispensable environment. The book will feature the method involved with making cradlesongs enlivened by the Cold's bedtime songs, underscoring the significance of bringing issues to light and elevating endeavors to safeguard this delicate climate.

1. Brief Overview of the Arctic

The Icy, a huge and puzzling domain, is one of the World's most enamoring but least grasped locales. Situated at the northernmost limit of our planet, this polar wild traverses across the Cold Sea, incorporating the northern pieces of a few nations, including Canada, Russia, the US (The Frozen North), Greenland (an independent domain of Denmark), Norway, Sweden, Finland, and Iceland. While the Icy might bring out pictures of destruction and outrageous cold, it is a place that is known for unrivaled normal magnificence, a residing demonstration of the planet's sensitive equilibrium. This article gives a complete outline of the Icy, investigating its topography, environment, remarkable biological systems, native societies, and the difficulties it faces in a period of quickly evolving environment.

1. **Topography**

   The Cold is portrayed by its super northern area, and its limits are not restricted to a solitary expanse of land but instead characterized by the Icy Circle, which is the southernmost line at which the sun stays apparent for a nonstop 24 hours throughout the mid year solstice and totally vanishes throughout the colder time of year solstice. This line fills in as an unpleasant division of the Icy district, reaching out to roughly 66.5 degrees north scope.

   Icy Sea

   The Cold Sea, a tremendous breadth of freezing waters, overwhelms the district. It is the littlest and shallowest of the world's seas and covers roughly 14 million square kilometers (5.4 million square miles).

   The Icy Sea is almost totally encircled via land, with just the Bering Waterway associating it to the Pacific Sea. This seclusion, joined with the presence of the encompassing mainlands, shapes the Cold's interesting environment and biological systems.

   Cold Body of land

   The Cold body of land comprises of a few nations and domains, including the northernmost districts of Canada, Russia, the US (The Frozen North), Greenland (an independent region of Denmark), Norway, Sweden, Finland, and Iceland.

   The Cold land region is covered by a different scope of conditions, including tundra, boreal woods, mountain ranges, and broad shores.

   Ice Cap and Glacial masses

   The Icy is described by huge ice sheets, icy masses, and ice covers, which contain an expected 90% of the world's freshwater ice. The Greenland Ice Sheet, specifically, is the second-biggest ice body on The planet, after the Antarctic Ice Sheet.

   These ice developments assume an essential part in the planet's environment guideline and are a crucial part of the World's freshwater cycle.

2. Environment

   The Icy is inseparable from outrageous cool, however its environment is undeniably more intricate than simply cold temperatures. The locale encounters critical varieties in environment consistently, formed by its one of a kind topographical and air conditions.

Polar Environment

The Icy is portrayed by a polar environment, with incredibly cool temperatures during the long cold weather months. Winters are dull and extreme, with temperatures falling great beneath freezing, frequently coming to - 40 degrees Celsius (- 40 degrees Fahrenheit).

The district encounters a short, cool summer portrayed by the well known 12 PM sun, during which the sun doesn't set for a long time.

Ocean Ice

Ocean ice covers a critical piece of the Cold Sea, extending and contracting with the evolving seasons. Throughout the colder time of year, ocean ice reaches out over huge regions, while in the late spring, it withdraws, leaving pockets of untamed water.

The degree and thickness of Icy ocean ice have been diminishing throughout the course of recent a very long time because of environmental change, with significant ramifications for both the Cold biological system and worldwide environment designs.

Permafrost

Permafrost, or forever frozen ground, is a characterizing element of the Cold scene. It exists underneath the surface and assumes a basic part in forming the district's hydrology and environments.

Environmental change has prompted the defrosting of permafrost, delivering ozone harming substances like methane and carbon dioxide into the climate, adding to a worldwide temperature alteration.

3. **Special Environments**

The Cold is home to many extraordinary and strong biological systems, adjusted to its outrageous environment and conditions.

Tundra

The Icy tundra is portrayed by huge stretches of treeless, low-lying vegetation, where the dirt is forever frozen and the developing season is short.

Regardless of its cruel circumstances, the tundra upholds a variety of plant and creature life, including notorious species like caribou, Icy rabbits, and muskoxen.

Boreal Backwoods

In the southern pieces of the Cold, especially in locales of Canada and Russia, boreal backwoods reach out into the polar zone. These woods comprise of cold-adjusted trees like tidy, fir, and pine.

The boreal timberlands give significant environment to different bird species and warm blooded creatures, including the subtle Siberian tiger.

Marine Environments

The Cold Sea supports an exceptional marine biological system, with species like the polar bear, walrus, beluga whale, and narwhal, which are uniquely adjusted to the outrageous circumstances.

Ocean ice is a vital stage for these creatures, filling in as a hunting ground for seals and a rearing site for birds.

Freshwater Environments

The Icy has various lakes, waterways, and wetlands, a considerable lot of which are taken care of by dissolving ice and permafrost. These freshwater environments are fundamental for the district's biodiversity.

Salmon, Icy roast, and a wide assortment of waterfowl possess these environments.

4. **Native Societies**

The Icy isn't simply a wild; likewise home to various native societies have adjusted to its requesting conditions over centuries.

Inuit

The Inuit are a gathering of native people groups who principally occupy the Icy districts of Canada, Greenland, The Frozen North, and Siberia. They have a rich social legacy and a profound association with the land and ocean.

Inuit people group depend on customary information to explore and make due in the Cold, and their lifestyle is firmly entwined with the climate.

Saami

The Saami, otherwise called the Sami, are the native individuals of northern Scandinavia, including portions of Norway, Sweden, Finland, and Russia. They have a profound association with the Cold's boreal timberlands and tundra.

The Saami have an interesting social personality, with an emphasis on reindeer grouping and the safeguarding of their conventional dialects.

Other Native Gatherings

The Cold is home to a variety of native gatherings, each with its remarkable practices, dialects, and lifestyles. These incorporate the Aleut, Chukchi, and Yupik people groups in The Frozen North, as well as the Nenets and Evenki in Russia.

5. **Difficulties and Preservation**

The Cold faces a huge number of difficulties, a considerable lot of which are exacerbated by the impacts of environmental change.

Environmental Change

The most major problem in the Icy is environmental change. Increasing temperatures are causing the quick dissolving of ocean ice, defrosting permafrost, and disturbing the locale's environments.

These progressions have significant ramifications for Cold untamed life, including the famous polar bear, which depends on ocean ice for hunting.

Contamination

Contamination, including plastics, weighty metals, and relentless natural poisons, represents a danger to Icy environments and untamed life. Pollutants gather in the established pecking order, influencing the two creatures and human networks.

The distance of the Cold doesn't safeguard it from the outcomes of contamination, as synthetic compounds can be moved significant distances through air and sea flows.

Asset Extraction

The Cold is plentiful in regular assets, including oil, gas, minerals, and fisheries. The scramble for asset extraction represents a gamble to the climate and native societies.

Offsetting monetary interests with preservation is a complicated test, and dependable asset the executives is significant.

Transportation and Framework

The contracting of Cold ocean ice is opening up new transportation courses and the potential for expanded human movement in the area.

This presents the two valuable open doors for financial turn of events and difficulties for protection, as expanded delivery traffic and framework improvement can upset untamed life and disturb customary lifestyles.

B. Importance of Arctic Wildlife

The Cold, frequently alluded to as the "Last Wilderness," is a district of unrivaled normal excellence and natural importance. It includes immense spreads of ice and tundra, and is home to a novel and various cluster of untamed life. While the Cold might appear to be remote and unfriendly to human existence, it is an indispensable piece of the worldwide environment. The untamed life that occupies this unforgiving climate assumes a pivotal part in keeping up with the sensitive equilibrium of our planet's environments. In this paper, we will investigate the significance of Cold natural life and the numerous manners by which it influences the world.

Biodiversity and Transformations

The Icy is home to an amazing assortment of untamed life species, every one of which has advanced remarkable transformations to make due in this cruel climate. From polar bears to icy foxes, and from walruses to narwhals, these animals have created particular qualities that permit them to flourish in a district where outrageous chilly, long winters, and restricted food assets are the standard.

The biodiversity of Icy untamed life isn't just a demonstration of the versatility of life yet additionally a wellspring of important hereditary variety. These variations can give experiences and answers for difficulties in different areas of the planet. For instance, researchers concentrating on Icy species have found qualities that assist creatures with enduring outrageous cold, which might actually be utilized to foster cold-safe harvests or work on how we might interpret human cold resistance.

Worldwide Environment Guideline

The Cold assumes a crucial part in managing the World's environment. The intelligent surfaces of ocean ice and snow help to bob daylight back into space, which affects the planet. This peculiarity, known as the albedo impact, assists with controlling worldwide temperatures and check the warming brought about by the nursery impact.

Cold untamed life, like polar bears and seals, are straightforwardly subject to the presence of ocean ice for hunting and rearing. As the ice liquefies because of environmental change, these species are in danger. This interruption to the Cold environment can have expansive ramifications for the whole planet. Less ice cover implies less impression of daylight, prompting expanded assimilation of intensity by the sea, which thusly speeds up an Earth-wide temperature boost. This positive input circle can have disastrous ramifications for the whole world, making the preservation of Icy untamed life and their territories urgent for environment guideline.

Natural Interconnections

Cold natural life is interconnected in complex ways, framing a sensitive trap of life. For example, tiny fish and green growth in the Icy Sea are the essential makers, framing the foundation of the pecking order. Zooplankton feed on these essential makers, and they, thusly, become prey for fish, which are pursued via seals, whales, and polar bears. These connections feature the significance of protecting the Cold's biodiversity to keep up with the equilibrium of its environments.

Cold natural life additionally relocates to different regions of the planet, further underlining their job in worldwide biological systems. For example, many bird species that variety in the Cold travel south throughout the colder time of year, spreading the seeds of Icy plants to distant locales. These movements give supplements to different biological systems and impact the hereditary variety of species in far off areas.

Social Importance

The Cold isn't just a position of natural significance yet additionally holds tremendous social incentive for native networks. For a really long time, the native people groups of the Cold, like the Inuit, Yupik, and Sami, have relied upon Icy untamed life for their means, culture, and lifestyle. These people group have a profound association with the land and creatures of the Cold, and their conventional information has been fundamental for understanding and moderating the district's biological systems.

The hunting and fishing practices of native people groups have been economical for ages, as they have a significant regard for the creatures and biological systems they depend on. Saving Cold natural life isn't just about safeguarding the climate yet additionally about protecting the social legacy and customs of native networks.

Logical Exploration

The Icy fills in as a characteristic research facility for researchers to concentrate on the impacts of environmental change and grasp the intricacies of biological systems. As the area encounters probably the most emotional effects of environmental change, it gives important experiences into the outcomes of a worldwide temperature alteration in the world. Specialists concentrate on Icy untamed life to screen the soundness of the biological system, survey the impacts of contamination, and research the transformation and methods for surviving of these species.

The discoveries from Cold examination have more extensive ramifications for understanding environmental change, biodiversity misfortune, and biological system elements on a worldwide scale. By safeguarding Cold natural life, we guarantee that this significant wellspring of information stays open to researchers and adds to how we might interpret the World's evolving climate.

Financial Worth

Cold natural life additionally has monetary importance, as it upholds different enterprises, like ecotourism, fisheries, and hunting. Travelers from around the world are attracted to the Icy to observe its shocking scenes and one of a kind untamed life. The income created from these exercises upholds neighborhood economies and protection endeavors.

The fishing business in the Icy is one more key monetary player, giving food and pay to neighborhood networks and worldwide business sectors. Economical administration of Icy fisheries is fundamental to guarantee that these assets are not overexploited and that the biological systems stay sound.

Moreover, the significance of Cold natural life reaches out to hunting. Native people group depend on chasing after means and social practices. This training has been a fundamental piece of their lifestyle for ages and keeps on being an essential part of their financial prosperity.

Protection of Jeopardized Species

The Icy is home to a few animal groups that are viewed as imperiled or powerless, including the polar bear, the narwhal, and the Cold fox. The preservation of these species is fundamental for their endurance as well as for the general strength of the environment. Polar bears, for instance, are at the head of the Icy pecking order and assume a urgent part in directing prey populaces. Their downfall can have flowing consequences for the whole biological system.

Endeavors to safeguard and moderate these species have more extensive ramifications for preservation overall. The techniques and procedures produced for Icy natural life protection can be applied to different districts and species confronting comparative difficulties. Consequently, the Cold fills in as a proving ground for preservation rehearses that can be utilized worldwide.

Security Against Intrusive Species

The brutal and distant climate of the Cold has, up to this point, filled in as a characteristic boundary to obtrusive species. Nonetheless, as the environment warms and human action in the district builds, the gamble of obtrusive species being presented develops. These intrusive species can disturb the sensitive equilibrium of Cold biological systems and undermine local greenery.

By saving the territories and environments of Cold untamed life, we can help safeguard against the spread of obtrusive species. Saving the Icy's novel biodiversity is fundamental for keeping up with the district's natural respectability.

Environment Administrations

Cold biological systems give a scope of environment benefits that benefit the worldwide local area. The carbon stockpiling limit of Icy tundra and peatlands mitigates environmental change overwhelmingly of carbon. As the environment warms, the arrival of put away carbon could additionally speed up an unnatural weather change, making the protection of Cold natural life significantly more basic.

Furthermore, the Cold assumes a significant part in the worldwide water cycle. The liquefying of Cold ice adds to rising ocean levels, which has suggestions for waterfront networks around the world. Also, the Icy directs sea flows and air dissemination, affecting weather conditions across the planet. These biological system administrations are fundamental for keeping up with worldwide environment strength and territorial weather conditions.

Moral and Moral Contemplations

Finally, the significance of Cold natural life can't be completely perceived disregarding the moral and moral parts of preservation. As overseers of the planet, people have an ethical obligation to safeguard and save the world's biodiversity. This obligation reaches out to the exceptional and weak species that possess the Icy.

The deficiency of Icy natural life wouldn't just address a disappointment of stewardship yet in addition mirror a dismissal for the characteristic worth of every single living being. Each specie plays a part in the excellent embroidery of life, and we should perceive and regard their entitlement to exist.

C. Purpose of the Book

Books hold a special and cherished place in our reality, filling in as conductors of information, creative mind, and human articulation. Each book has a reason, an unmistakable justification for its creation, whether it be to engage, illuminate, rouse, incite thought, or even test shows. The motivation behind a book is a crucial perspective that directs the writer's expectations and shapes the peruser's insight. In this investigation of the reason for a book, we dig into the diverse jobs that writing plays in our lives and society, recognizing its significant effect on culture, information, and the human experience.

To Illuminate and Teach

One of the basic roles of books is to illuminate and instruct. Verifiable books, scholarly texts, and reference materials are made to share information, research discoveries, and bits of knowledge with perusers. These books act as supplies of realities, information, and examination, permitting people to extend how they might interpret different subjects.

Course books, for instance, assume a vital part in conventional schooling, assisting understudies with embracing complex ideas and gain skill in unambiguous fields. Verifiable records, accounts, and journals give bits of knowledge into the past, permitting perusers to gain from the encounters of others. Logical distributions offer the most recent revelations and headways, propelling human comprehension of the normal world.

To Engage and Get away

Books frequently act for the purpose of amusement and idealism. Books, brief tales, and verse transport perusers to various universes, acquainting them with enthralling characters, exciting experiences, and creative settings. These works of fiction offer a departure from the commonplace, giving snapshots of euphoria, tension, or even therapy.

Creators make stories that resound with our feelings and wants, assisting us with briefly backing away from the intricacies of our own lives. Whether it's an exhilarating secret, an endearing sentiment, or an arresting sci-fi epic, these books act as vehicles for diversion, empowering us to unwind and loosen up.

To Move and Spur

Books can be strong wellsprings of motivation and inspiration. They frequently include genuine records of people who have beaten misfortune, accomplished significance, or had a tremendous effect on the world. These accounts act as a wellspring of expectation and support for perusers confronting difficulties in their own lives.

Life stories and collections of memoirs of momentous figures, like Mahatma Gandhi, Nelson Mandela, and Malala Yousafzai, motivate perusers to seek after their objectives, defend their convictions, and have a beneficial outcome on the planet. Self improvement and self-awareness books give methodologies to personal growth, offering direction on making individual and expert progress.

To Save Culture and History

Books assume a fundamental part in saving society and history. They report the encounters, convictions, and customs of various social orders, guaranteeing that the information and legacy of past ages are not lost. Verifiable records, oral accounts, and social stories are sent through the composed word, adding to the aggregate memory of mankind.

Fictitious works set in unambiguous verifiable periods, as dickens Charles' "A Story of Two Urban communities," transport perusers to various periods, giving a brief look into the cultural standards and difficulties of the time. Books likewise assist us with gaining from the mix-ups and accomplishments of the past, filling in as tokens of our common history and the illustrations it offers.

To Cultivate Decisive Reasoning and Discussion

A few books are made with the goal of cultivating decisive reasoning and discussion. These works frequently challenge laid out standards, philosophies, or winning suppositions. Creators might utilize writing to incite thought, energize discourse, and go up against cultural issues that request consideration and change.

Tragic books, for example, as orwell George's "1984" or Aldous Huxley's "State-of-the-art existence," act as wake up calls, encouraging perusers to consider the outcomes of tyranny and the disintegration of individual opportunities. Philosophical messages, papers, and pugnacious writing present assorted perspectives on complex points, advancing basic examination and conversations.

To Convey Individual or Social Stories

Books are a mode for sharing individual stories and social stories. Journals, self-portrayals, and family backgrounds permit people to share their extraordinary encounters, battles, and wins with a more extensive crowd. These stories offer understanding into the creator's life, revealing insight into their points of view, feelings, and self-awareness.

Social stories, then again, give a stage to underrepresented voices and viewpoints. These books assist with connecting social partitions, bring issues to light of assorted encounters, and support compassion and understanding. They add to a rich embroidery of human stories that enhance our worldwide local area.

To Investigate Complex Feelings and Connections

Writing frequently dives into the intricacies of human feelings and connections. Books and verse investigate subjects of adoration, companionship, treachery, melancholy, and innumerable different parts of the human condition. Writers utilize their work to give knowledge into the complexities of the human mind, causing perusers to ponder their own sentiments and associations with others.

Works of art as austen Jane's "Pride and Bias" or Leo Tolstoy's "Anna Karenina" inspect the subtleties of close connections, cultural assumptions, and self-awareness. By diving into these subjects, writing offers a mirror through which perusers can all the more likely grasp their own close to home encounters.

To Advance Compassion and Understanding

Books have the ability to advance sympathy and understanding by permitting perusers to step into the shoes of characters from different foundations and encounters. Through writing, perusers can acquire knowledge into the existences of individuals who are not the same as themselves, encouraging a feeling of compassion and resistance.

Books that address social issues, like prejudice, disparity, and segregation, set out a freedom for perusers to face these issues according to different points of view. Stories that investigate the encounters of minimized networks assist with combatting generalizations, challenge predispositions, and empower social change.

To Mirror the Human Condition

One of the most profound motivations behind books is to mirror the human condition. Writing catches the embodiment of being human, with every one of our assets, shortcomings, and logical inconsistencies. Writers make characters and stories that resound with perusers on a significant level, featuring the common parts of the human experience.

Books as dostoevsky Fyodor's "Wrongdoing and Discipline" or Gabriel García Márquez's "100 Years of Isolation" dig into subjects of profound quality, culpability, and the intricacy of human instinct. By tending to these widespread parts of the human condition, writing turns into a mirror that assists perusers with figuring out their own lives.

To Animate Creative mind and Innovativeness

Creative mind and imagination are fundamental components of the human soul, and books assume an essential part in animating these resources. Fiction, dream, and sci-fi classes transport perusers to conjured up universes, empowering them to investigate novel thoughts and conceivable outcomes.

Youngsters' books, like crafted by Dr. Seuss or Roald Dahl, light the minds of youthful perusers, moving them to dream, imagine, and imagine a universe of vast potential outcomes. Additionally, sci-fi books as asimov Isaac's "Establishment" challenge perusers to consider the capability of innovation and the fate of humankind.

To Offer Comfort and Solace

Books have the ability to give comfort and solace during troublesome times. Works that address subjects of misfortune, despondency, and mending can offer a feeling of friendship to the people who are battling. Perusers frequently find comfort in the expressions of creators who have confronted comparable difficulties and arisen with astuteness and strength.

Self improvement and uplifting writing, like Viktor E. Frankl's "Man's Quest for Significance," offer direction and solace to people managing individual emergencies. These books give bits of knowledge on tracking down significance in affliction and exploring life's most significant difficulties.

To Challenge and Grow Limits

A few books are made with the particular aim of pushing the limits of writing and thought. Trial writing, vanguard works, and offbeat narrating challenge customary standards and assumptions. They try to extend the potential outcomes of what writing can accomplish.

Creators like James Joyce, with his momentous book "Ulysses," and Virginia Woolf, with her continuous flow accounts, have tried the constraints of story construction and language. These books urge perusers to draw in with writing in new and imaginative ways, pushing the limits of narrating and human articulation.

To Backer for Social Change

Books have a long history of supporting for social change and equity. Scholars frequently utilize their fills in as stages to reveal insight into cultural issues and rouse activity. Whether through fiction or true to life, books can bring issues to light, flash developments, and drive progress.

Harriet Beecher Stowe's "Uncle Tom's Lodge" assumed an essential part in the abolitionist development, encouraging perusers to stand up to the repulsions of subjection and request its end. All the more as of late, books like Ta-Nehisi Coates' "Between the World and Me" have lighted discussions about race and imbalance, filling in as impetuses for social change.

To Record Individual Encounters and Viewpoints

Each individual's life is an extraordinary excursion, and certain individuals decide to record their encounters through books. Diaries, journals, and individual papers give a method for recording individual stories, reflections, and points of view. These works offer bits of knowledge into the creator's viewpoints, feelings, and the occasions that have formed their lives.

Individual stories can be seriously interesting, offering perusers the chance to interface with the creator on a profoundly private level. Whether it's Anne Straight to the point's journal or the individual expositions of Joan Didion, these compositions give a brief look into the existences of others and proposition a feeling of closeness and association.

To Make Workmanship and Magnificence

Books are show-stoppers in themselves. The magnificence of language, the force of narrating, and the craftsmanship of book configuration add to the stylish allure of writing. The motivation behind certain books is essentially to make workmanship and magnificence, to charm the faculties, and to rouse appreciation for the composed word.

Verse is a perfect representation of writing as craftsmanship, where language is made into reminiscent and melodic structures. Crafted by writers like William Shakespeare, Emily Dickinson, and Pablo Neruda convey significant feelings as well as exhibit the creativity of words and articulation.

Chapter 1

The Icy Wonderland

The polar districts, enveloping the Icy in the north and the Antarctic in the south, are the absolute most limit and perfect conditions on The planet. These frosty wonderlands, described by tremendous regions of snow and ice, cold temperatures, and novel environments, hold an extraordinary spot in our aggregate creative mind. In this investigation of the polar areas, we will dig into their normal excellence, natural importance, and the difficulties they face in a period of environmental change.

Icy and Antarctic: Particular Universes

To start our excursion into the frosty wonderlands, understanding the qualification between the Cold and Antarctic regions is fundamental. While they share a few similitudes, they are, truth be told, two isolated and particular universes.

The Icy: The Icy is situated in the Northern Side of the equator and encompasses the Icy Sea. It incorporates the Icy Sea itself, as well as the northern pieces of North America (Gold country and Canada), Europe (Scandinavian nations), and Asia (Russia). It's described by the presence of ocean ice, permafrost, and a blend of land and water.

The Antarctic: The Antarctic, then again, is arranged in the Southern Side of the equator and envelops the landmass of Antarctica, which is encircled by the Southern Sea. Not at all like the Cold, the Antarctic is a landmass encircled by water. It highlights transcending ice sheets and icy masses, with the South Pole at its middle.

While the two districts experience outrageous chilly, long polar evenings, and remarkable untamed life, they vary in their geology, environment, and biological systems. The Cold is described by a blend of land and ocean, with a moving ice cover, while the Antarctic is an enormous expanse of land primarily covered by ice.

Polar Environments: Transformations to Limits

The polar districts are home to a striking exhibit of untamed life, in spite of their unforgiving circumstances. Life in these frigid conditions has developed novel transformations that permit species to flourish in the super cold and seclusion. These transformations include:

Thick Protection: Numerous polar creatures have advanced thick layers of lard or fur to protect their bodies and safeguard them from the virus. Species like polar bears, seals, and walruses depend on these variations to keep up with their body heat in bone chilling waters.

Counter-Current Intensity Trade: A few creatures, for example, penguins, utilize a counter-current intensity trade framework in their legs to forestall heat misfortune to the encompassing ice. This empowers them to swim in frigid waters without losing an excess of body heat.

Adapting to Haziness: In polar districts, the winters are set apart by extensive stretches of dimness. Creatures in these locales have adjusted to this by creating elevated detects, like prevalent night vision and sharp feelings of smell and hearing. They utilize these faculties to find prey and explore their current circumstance in obscurity.

Disguise: Numerous species have developed a white or dim tinge to mix in with the frigid scenes. This assists them with keeping away from hunters or remain concealed while hunting.

Movement and Hibernation: A few creatures in the Cold, similar to caribou and Icy terns, relocate significant distances to track down food and breed in additional ideal circumstances. Conversely, certain species sleep during the brutal cold weather months, monitoring energy until conditions get to the next level.

Specific Weight control plans: Species like the Cold fox and frigid owl have adjusted to their current circumstance by advancing particular eating regimens that incorporate little warm blooded creatures and birds. These food sources are accessible all year and give the energy expected to endurance.

Liquid catalyst Proteins: Numerous polar fish and spineless creatures have radiator fluid proteins in their blood, which keep ice precious stones from framing inside their bodies, guaranteeing they don't freeze in the freezing waters.

The variety of transformations among polar species is a demonstration of the versatility of life on our planet. It likewise highlights the interconnectedness of biological systems, as every species assumes an exceptional part in the snare of life.

Cold Biological systems

The Cold, with its blend of land and ocean, is home to a rich exhibit of environments, including the tundra, boreal timberlands, and the Icy Sea. These biological systems are interwoven and support various plant and creature species.

Tundra Environment: The Icy tundra is a tremendous, treeless district with a short developing season because of its super virus. It is home to greeneries, lichens, and low-lying bushes. During the short summer, it blasts into existence with wildflowers. Transitory birds, caribou, reindeer, and muskoxen are among the species that depend on the tundra for their endurance.

Boreal Backwoods: The northern spans of the Cold, especially in Canada and Russia, contain boreal woodlands, otherwise called taiga. These backwoods comprise of coniferous trees like tidy, pine, and fir. Natural life in this locale incorporates moose, wolves, lynx, and an assortment of bird animal types.

Icy Sea Biological system: The Cold Sea is overflowing with life, from minuscule phytoplankton to huge marine vertebrates like whales, seals, and walruses. Ocean ice gives a stage to seals to rest and conceive an offspring, and it upholds zooplankton, which are an essential food hotspot for fish and marine warm blooded creatures.

Polar Desert: The high Icy locales, like those tracked down in the Canadian Archipelago, are delegated polar deserts because of their very dry circumstances. Notwithstanding this, the locale has different types of natural life, including the Icy bunny and lemmings.

Seaside and Marine Environments: The Icy's shorelines are basic natural surroundings for an assortment of bird animal categories, including puffins, guillemots, and eiders. Furthermore, the kelp woodlands found in Icy waters give asylum and food to various marine species.

Antarctic Environments

Antarctica, with its broad ice sheets and brutal environment, is a place that is known for limits. Regardless of its apparently unwelcoming conditions, it upholds an astonishing variety of life, especially in its beach front districts.

Waterfront Environments: The banks of Antarctica are the most naturally dynamic regions on the mainland. Here, penguins, seals, and seabirds assemble to raise and take care of. The supplement rich waters of the Southern Sea support a wealth of krill, which shapes the premise of the Antarctic food web.

Inland Dry Valleys: The Dry Valleys of Antarctica are quite possibly of the driest put on The planet, getting just insignificant precipitation. However, microbial life can be seen as here, where the scene looks like a Martian landscape. The presence of life in these outrageous circumstances has suggestions for the quest for life on different planets.

Underneath the Ice: Underneath the thick ice sheets, there are subglacial lakes that have been detached from the rest of the world for a long period of time. In spite of the super cold and murkiness, researchers have found microbial life in these secret biological systems, showing life's capacity to adjust to the most outrageous conditions.

Marine Life: The freezing waters of the Southern Sea are abounding with life, including seals, whales, and fish. The yearly blast of phytoplankton in the late spring upholds a different local area of krill, which, thusly, gives food to bigger marine creatures.

The polar biological systems are of extraordinary environmental importance, for their special variations as well as for the job they play in worldwide environment guideline.

Environment Guideline and Worldwide Effect

The polar locales assume a crucial part in directing the World's environment. A few critical cycles and input circles make them necessary to keeping up with worldwide environment steadiness:

Albedo Impact: One of the main environment guideline elements of the polar districts is the albedo impact. Snow and ice reflect daylight back into space, keeping the Earth cooler. This intelligent nature of ice and snow is pivotal in counterbalancing the warming brought about by the nursery impact.

Worldwide Flows: The virus waters around Antarctica and the Icy assist with driving worldwide sea flows. The sinking of chilly, thick water in these areas starts the flow of sea flows, which heft heat all over the world and impact environment designs around the world.

Carbon Capacity: The polar areas store immense amounts of carbon in permafrost and ice. As the environment warms, this put away carbon is in danger of being delivered into the air, adding to the nursery impact and further warming the planet.

Ocean Level Guideline: The softening of polar ice adds to rising ocean levels. The polar locales go about as a characteristic indoor regulator, assisting with directing ocean levels and safeguard beach front regions.

The destiny of the polar districts is complicatedly connected to worldwide environmental change. The effects of environmental change are felt more intensely here than in most different regions of the planet.

As temperatures increase, polar ice is softening at a sped up rate, with huge ramifications for the World's environment framework and biological systems.

Environmental Change and Its Belongings

Environmental change represents an impressive test to the polar districts, with significant ramifications for their biological systems, untamed life, and the planet all in all:

Fast Ice Dissolve: Both the Cold and Antarctic are encountering quick ice soften, bringing about the deficiency of ocean ice, ice sheets, and ice racks. This adds to rising ocean levels as well as disturbs environments that depend on these ice arrangements.

Changing Sea Dissemination: Warming waters in the polar districts can upset the worldwide course of sea flows, which significantly affect weather conditions. Changes in these flows can prompt outrageous climate occasions in far off districts.

Loss of Territory: Polar bears, seals, penguins, and numerous different species are losing their regular environments because of ice misfortune and temperature changes. This affects the whole pecking order, as these species rely upon ice for hunting and rearing.

Arrival of Methane: As permafrost in the Icy defrosts, it can deliver methane, a powerful ozone depleting substance, into the climate. Methane discharges further compound a worldwide temperature alteration.

Marine Biological system Disturbance: Sea fermentation, driven by expanded carbon dioxide levels, influences marine life in the polar districts. This has repercussions for the endurance of species that depend on calcium carbonate for their shells, like specific sorts of phytoplankton.

Expanded Transportation and Asset Extraction: As ice retreats in the Cold, new delivery courses and open doors for asset extraction have arisen. While this has financial ramifications, it additionally conveys the gamble of contamination, territory annihilation, and possible struggles over assets.

Dangers to Native People group: Environmental change represents an immediate danger to the customary lifestyles of native networks in the polar districts. Changing atmospheric conditions and softening ice influence their capacity to chase, fish, and keep up with their social practices.

Endeavors to relieve the impacts of environmental change in the polar districts are essential for the prosperity of the planet. Peaceful accords and exploration drives expect to address the difficulties confronting the polar locales and advance manageable practices.

Protection and Conservation

The protection and conservation of the polar districts are fundamental not just for the prosperity of the environments and untamed life that call these regions home yet additionally for the dependability of the worldwide environment framework. Preservation endeavors include a few key techniques:

Safeguarding Key Species: The protection of notable species like polar bears, penguins, and seals is a focal point of preservation endeavors. Safeguarding their territories and food sources is fundamental for their endurance.

Marine Safeguarded Regions: Laying out marine safeguarded regions helps shield crucial taking care of and favorable places for marine species. These regions can likewise decrease the effect of delivery and asset extraction on polar biological systems.

Decreasing Ozone depleting substance Outflows: One of the main moves toward safeguard the polar districts is diminishing ozone depleting substance discharges. Worldwide endeavors to control discharges and progress to sustainable power sources are basic for alleviating environmental change.

Advancing Supportable Practices: Manageable the travel industry and examination rehearses in the polar locales can limit the ecological effect of human exercises. Dependable the travel industry, including rules for natural life experiences and garbage removal, is vital.

Supporting Native People group: Native people group in the polar districts are frequently at the very front of preservation endeavors. Supporting these networks and regarding their conventional information is essential for the progress of protection drives.

Logical Exploration: Exploration assumes a urgent part in understanding the effects of environmental change on the polar districts and creating systems to moderate these impacts. Logical review is fundamental for informed navigation and preservation endeavors.

The polar locales are confronting significant difficulties, however they likewise offer an encouraging sign. By understanding the significance of these areas and making a move to safeguard them, we can add to the conservation of their remarkable biological systems and the strength of our planet's environment.

The Frigid Wonderland and Our Aggregate Liability

The polar locales, with their dazzling scenes, novel biological systems, and basic jobs in environment guideline, are normal ponders that catch the creative mind of individuals all over the planet. Their excellence and importance help us to remember the grandness of our planet and the significance of capable stewardship.

As we investigate the frosty wonderlands of the Cold and Antarctic, it becomes clear that these districts are both delicate and strong. They are delicate despite fast environmental change, yet strong because of the variations of their occupants and the interconnectedness of their biological systems.

Our aggregate liability lies in saving and safeguarding these districts, not just for the polar untamed life yet for the prosperity of all life on The planet. By making a move to relieve environmental change, support protection endeavors, and regard the customary information on native networks, we can guarantee that the frigid wonderlands proceed to charm and motivate ages to come. The polar districts, in the entirety of their magnificence and difficulties, coax us to move toward a practical and amicable conjunction with the normal world.

1.1 Introduction to the Arctic Environment

The Icy, frequently depicted as the "last outskirts," is an immense and mysterious district situated at the northernmost piece of our planet. This remarkable climate, portrayed by outrageous chilly, dazzling scenes, and a sensitive natural equilibrium, assumes a basic part in the worldwide environment framework. In this prologue to the Cold climate, we will investigate the key highlights, difficulties, and meaning of this remote and wonderful area of the planet.

Topography and Environment:

The Cold envelops the northern polar area, including the Icy Sea, portions of Gold country, Canada, Greenland, Scandinavia, Russia, and the Icy archipelago. This immense field traverses around 14 million square kilometers and is frequently partitioned into two particular districts: the Cold Sea and the land-based Icy.

One of the characterizing elements of the Cold is its cruel environment, with freezing temperatures and expanded times of murkiness in the colder time of year. The Icy is known for its super cold, with temperatures that can plunge to - 40°C (- 40°F) or lower. On the other hand, during the concise late spring months, temperatures can climb to simply above freezing, considering an explosion of life and movement in this generally frozen scene.

Novel Highlights of the Icy Climate:

The Icy's remarkable climate is described by a few particular highlights:

Polar Ice:

The Cold is eminent for broad ocean ice covers the Icy Sea. Throughout the colder time of year, this ice cap develops, almost multiplying the locale's size, prior to retreating in the late spring. The ice fills in as a critical natural surroundings for various species, including polar bears and seals, and assumes a huge part in directing the World's environment.

Permafrost:

A significant part of the Icy's expanse of land is underlain by permafrost, which is soil that stays frozen over time. This frozen layer can expand a few meters down and significantly affects the locale's biological systems and foundation.

Biodiversity:

As opposed to prevalent thinking, the Cold is definitely not an inert no man's land. It is home to a shockingly different scope of widely varied vegetation, adjusted to the outrageous circumstances. Notorious species like polar bears, reindeer, and Icy foxes meander this locale, and transient birds utilize the Cold as a favorable place.

Aurora Borealis:

The Icy is renowned for its dazzling light presentation, the Aurora Borealis or Aurora Borealis. These normal light shows are made by charged particles from the sun associating with the World's attractive field, bringing about bright and entrancing showcases in the Icy night skies.

Ecological Difficulties:

Notwithstanding its remote and immaculate appearance, the Cold faces a huge number of ecological difficulties, a considerable lot of which are exacerbated by environmental change. These difficulties include:

Softening Ocean Ice:

Increasing worldwide temperatures have prompted the fast decay of Icy ocean ice, which has serious ramifications for both neighborhood biological systems and the worldwide environment. Diminished ice inclusion influences the living space of marine species and adds to the ocean level ascent.

Defrosting Permafrost:

As temperatures increase, permafrost is defrosting, delivering long-caught ozone harming substances, like methane, into the climate. This input circle further speeds up a dangerous atmospheric devation.

Disintegration and Framework Harm:

The deficiency of ocean ice and defrosting permafrost have expanded waterfront disintegration in the Cold, compromising networks and foundation worked along the coastline.

Adjusted Environments:

Changing ecological circumstances are disturbing Icy biological systems, influencing the jobs of native networks and the species that depend on the district for endurance.

Asset Extraction:

The softening ice has opened up valuable open doors for asset extraction, including oil and gaseous petrol boring, which presents both financial open doors and ecological dangers.

Meaning of the Cold Climate:

The Icy assumes a basic part in the World's environment framework, and its ecological changes have expansive ramifications for the whole planet. Here are a few key motivations behind why the Cold climate is critical:

Worldwide Environment Guideline:

The Icy directs the World's environment by reflecting daylight and intensity back into space. At the point when the ice cover reduces, more intensity is ingested, adding to worldwide temperature increase.

Biodiversity Protection:

The Icy is home to remarkable and frequently imperiled species, making its protection pivotal for worldwide biodiversity.

Social Legacy:

Native people groups, like the Inuit and Saami, have occupied the Cold for centuries, and their societies are profoundly entwined with the climate. Safeguarding their conventional information and lifestyle is fundamental.

Logical Exploration:

The Cold gives a characteristic research facility to concentrating on environmental change, biological systems, and barometrical cycles. Experiences acquired from this locale are crucial for grasping worldwide ecological movements.

Asset The executives:

The Cold holds huge stores of minerals, oil, and petroleum gas, making it a significant region for asset the executives and worldwide collaboration.

1.2 Unique Features of the Arctic

The Cold is a locale of unrivaled normal excellence and outrageous circumstances. Its interesting elements put it aside from some other put on The planet and make it a really exceptional piece of our planet. In this investigation of the Icy's remarkable attributes, we will dig into the most particular angles that characterize this remote and spellbinding climate.

Polar Ice:

The most notorious component of the Icy is without a doubt its tremendous regions of polar ice. Throughout the colder time of year, the Icy Sea becomes canvassed in a thick layer of ocean ice, reaching out for a significant distance toward each path. This ice can arrive at a few meters in thickness and is a fundamental part of the Icy's biological system. It fills in as a living space for different species, including polar bears and seals, and goes about as a characteristic boundary, reflecting daylight and assisting with cooling the Earth.

Permafrost:

Permafrost is a characterizing topographical component of the Icy scene. Permafrost is soil that stays frozen all year, and it can expand far beneath the World's surface. The presence of permafrost significantly affects the district's biological systems, as it limits the profundity to which plants can root and influences the development of water.

Besides, permafrost stores a lot of carbon, and as it defrosts because of environmental change, it discharges ozone harming substances into the air, adding to an Earth-wide temperature boost.

Polar Evening and 12 PM Sun:

The Cold encounters outrageous varieties in sunlight over time. Throughout the colder time of year, a few region of the Icy are dove into a condition of interminable murkiness, known as the polar evening, for quite some time. On the other hand, in the mid year, the Icy encounters the peculiarity of the 12 PM sun, where the sun stays over the skyline for a lengthy period, frequently 24 hours every day. These special lighting conditions significantly influence the district's greenery, fauna, and human occupants, impacting their day to day rhythms and exercises.

Aurora Borealis (Aurora Borealis):

The Cold is eminent for the staggering normal light shows known as the Aurora Borealis or Aurora Borealis. These beautiful and hypnotizing peculiarities happen when charged particles from the sun associate with the World's attractive field. The subsequent light shows are a demonstration of the Icy's captivating magnificence and have for some time been a wellspring of marvel and motivation for the people who are sufficiently lucky to observe them.

Biodiversity:

In opposition to the impression of the Icy as a desolate no man's land, it is home to a shockingly different scope of species, large numbers of which have adjusted to the cruel circumstances. Notable creatures like the polar bear, Cold fox, reindeer, and different types of seals and whales occupy the area. Notwithstanding its marine and earthly fauna, the Cold backings an assortment of vegetation, especially during the short late spring months when the tundra blasts into dynamic sprout.

Cold Scenes:

The Cold is described by its emotional frosty scenes. Immense ice sheets and glacial masses cover a significant part of the land, chiseling tough mountain ranges, profound fjords, and sensational ice shelves. The constant development of these icy masses and the reshaping of the land are continuous geographical cycles that have helped shape the Cold's remarkable geography.

Outrageous Virus:

The Icy holds the record for the absolute coldest temperatures on The planet, with winter temperatures diving to - 40°C (- 40°F) or even lower. This super virus presents an impressive test to any living things occupying the district and expects them to foster exceptional transformations for endurance.

Novel Native Societies:

The Icy is home to different native networks, like the Inuit, Saami, and Yupik, who have created perplexing and feasible lifestyles firmly associated with the land and ocean. Their societies, customs, and dialects are a fundamental piece of the Cold's extraordinary embroidery.

In outline, the Icy's exceptional highlights consolidate to establish a stand-out climate that catches the creative mind and interest of individuals around the world. Its polar ice, permafrost, outrageous light varieties, Aurora Borealis, various biodiversity, icy scenes, outrageous cold, and energetic native societies all add to the Icy's unmistakable personality. As we proceed to study and value this exceptional locale, it turns out to be progressively certain that the Cold isn't simply a remote corner of the Earth yet a position of gigantic importance for both science and the protection of our worldwide biological system.

1.3 The Polar Night and Midnight Sun

The Cold, a locale known for its outrageous circumstances and novel highlights, encounters quite possibly of the most charming and momentous normal peculiarity on The planet: the Polar Evening and 12 PM Sun. These two heavenly occasions, portrayed by the drawn out obscurity of the Polar Evening and the consistent light of the 12 PM Sun, are the consequence of the World's hub slant and its circle around the sun. In this investigation, we will dive into the science, social importance, and the effect of the Polar Evening and 12 PM Sun on the Cold and its occupants.

Understanding the Polar Evening and 12 PM Sun:

The Polar Evening and 12 PM Sun are peculiarities that happen in districts situated inside or close to the Icy Circle, a fanciful line of scope roughly 66.5 degrees north of the equator. They are the immediate consequence of the World's pivotal slant, which is answerable for the evolving seasons. As the Earth circles the sun, various pieces of the planet get differing measures of daylight over time.

Polar Evening:

The Polar Evening, otherwise called the "Cold evening," is a period when the Icy district encounters consistent murkiness. It happens throughout the cold weather months when the North Pole slants from the sun, making the sun stay underneath the skyline for a drawn out span. The specific timing and length of the Polar Night change contingent upon the scope, with additional northern areas encountering longer times of haziness.

12 PM Sun:

Alternately, the 12 PM Sun, or the "Cold day," is the partner to the Polar Evening. It happens throughout the mid year months when the North Pole slants towards the sun, bringing about consistent light. The 12 PM Sun peculiarity is named for the way that the sun is noticeable over the skyline, even at 12 PM, and it frequently continues for a really long time or even months, contingent upon the particular area inside the Cold Circle.

The Science Behind the Peculiarities:

These heavenly occasions are an immediate outcome of the World's pivotal slant, which is roughly 23.5 degrees. As the Earth circles the sun, various areas get changing measures of daylight consistently. The pivotal slant guarantees that the polar locales, including the Cold, experience outrageous varieties in sunshine and dimness.

During the Polar Evening, the Icy district is shifted away from the sun, making the sun's beams be at a point excessively low to arrive at the area. Subsequently, the Icy is encompassed in constant obscurity, and how much sunlight turns out to be logically more limited the nearer one gets toward the North Pole.

On the other hand, during the 12 PM Sun, the Icy locale is shifted towards the sun, permitting the sun to stay over the skyline for a drawn out period. The degree and term of consistent light rely upon the scope, with additional northern areas encountering the 12 PM Sun for a more broadened period.

Social Importance:

The Polar Evening and 12 PM Sun have significant social importance for the networks and native people groups living in the Icy. These peculiarities have molded the customs, ways of life, and conviction frameworks of these populaces for quite a long time. Here are a few manners by which the Polar Evening and 12 PM Sun are socially significant:

Conventional Services and Festivities:

Numerous native networks in the Icy hold customary functions and celebrations to stamp the appearance of the 12 PM Sun or the finish of the Polar Evening. These occasions act as a chance for networks to meet up, celebrate, and reconnect with their social legacy.

Route and Timekeeping:

In districts where the 12 PM Sun goes on for a lengthy period, individuals have created remarkable techniques for exploring and keeping time. Conventional techniques like following the place of the sun or the stars are utilized to decide bearing and time.

Stories and Folklore:

The Polar Evening and 12 PM Sun have motivated various fantasies and legends in Cold societies. These accounts frequently connect with the heavenly occasions as well as the progressions in nature and untamed life that go with them.

Association with the Climate:

The Icy's native societies have major areas of strength for a to the land, ocean, and natural life. The appearance of the 12 PM Sun or the finish of the Polar Night frequently denotes the start of exercises like hunting, fishing, and assembling, which are fundamental for their customary lifestyle.

Workmanship and Imagination:

The Icy's novel lighting conditions during the Polar Evening and 12 PM Sun have impacted workmanship and imagination in the locale. Specialists frequently draw motivation from the ethereal nature of the light and the emotional changes in the regular scene.

Influence on Day to day existence:

The Polar Evening and 12 PM Sun fundamentally affect the day to day routines of individuals in the Cold. These peculiarities achieve the two difficulties and open doors:

Circadian Rhythms and Wellbeing:

The lengthy obscurity of the Polar Night can disturb individuals' circadian rhythms and rest designs, possibly prompting conditions like Occasional Full of feeling Issue (Miserable). On the other hand, the 12 PM Sun can influence rest designs and require changes in day to day schedules.

Monetary Exercises:

The appearance of the 12 PM Sun frequently denotes the start of the fishing season, which is a urgent monetary movement in the Cold. Likewise, the finish of the Polar Night can connote the resumption of hunting and other outside exercises.

The travel industry:

The extraordinary peculiarity of the 12 PM Sun draws in travelers from around the world who visit the Icy to observe this normal miracle. The Polar Evening, with its true capacity for aurora seeing, likewise attracts travelers trying to encounter the sorcery of Aurora Borealis.

Transport and Wellbeing:

The constant murkiness of the Polar Evening and the splendid light of the 12 PM Sun can influence transportation and security. Satisfactory lighting and route frameworks are important to guarantee safe travel during these super light circumstances.

1.4 How Climate Change is Affecting the Arctic

The Cold, a locale known for its dazzling scenes and novel highlights, is encountering the effects of environmental change at a disturbing rate. The impacts of an Earth-wide temperature boost are more articulated in the Cold than in most different regions of the planet, bringing about a quickly changing climate that has broad results for the actual Icy as well as for the whole planet. In this top to bottom investigation, we will analyze what environmental change is meaning for the Cold and the different biological, ecological, and cultural outcomes of these changes.

1. Fast Warming:

The most clear effect of environmental change in the Cold is the quick expansion in temperatures. Throughout recent many years, the Cold has warmed at over two times the pace of the worldwide normal. This warming pattern, known as Cold intensification, is a consequence of different input instruments. The retreat of profoundly intelligent ocean ice and the openness of hazier sea water, for instance, ingest more sun oriented energy, intensifying the warming impact.

The results of this warming are complex:

Dissolving Ice: The most apparent impact is the contracting of Icy ocean ice. The mid year ocean ice degree has been consistently diminishing, and more slender ice is more powerless to additional softening. This has desperate ramifications for the Icy environment and adds to rising ocean levels all around the world.

Defrosting Permafrost: Permafrost, which underlies a large part of the Icy's expanse of land, is likewise defrosting quickly. As permafrost dissolves, it discharges put away carbon and methane, strong ozone harming substances that speed up a dangerous atmospheric devation.

2. **Ocean Level Ascent:**

   The dissolving of Icy ice adds to worldwide ocean level ascent, representing a danger to beach front networks around the world. The rising ocean levels increment the gamble of beach front disintegration and flooding, influencing Icy people group as well as those living in lower-scope regions.

3. **Modified Biological systems:**

   The changing environment is significantly affecting Cold biological systems. The district's extraordinary greenery are encountering interruptions, with ramifications for biodiversity and pecking orders. A few key effects include:

   Loss of Environment: Contracting ocean ice influences the living space of marine species like polar bears, seals, and walruses, making it more trying for these creatures to chase and raise.

   Changes in Relocation Examples: Changes in ocean ice and sea temperatures are influencing the circulation and movement examples of fish species, which, thus, influence the accessibility of nourishment for marine warm blooded creatures and seabirds.

Hotter Waters: Hotter Icy waters are making it more provoking for cold-water species to get by, while intrusive species are extending their reach into the district.

Interruption of Tiny fish Blossoms: Dissolving ice carries all the more new water into the Cold Sea, which disturbs the timing and area of phytoplankton sprouts, a basic food hotspot for marine life.

4. **Influence on Native People group:**
Native people groups in the Cold, like the Inuit, Saami, and Yupik, have long depended on the area's assets for their conventional lifestyle. Environmental change is presenting huge difficulties to these networks, including:

Dangers to Food Security: Changing ice conditions and the relocation of key species like caribou and seals influence the accessibility of conventional food sources, prompting expanded food instability.

Disintegration and Foundation Harm: Beach front disintegration, exacerbated by the deficiency of ocean ice and defrosting permafrost, is affecting homes and framework in numerous native networks, prompting constrained movements.

Social Interruption: As the Cold climate changes, so too do the conventional information and practices of native networks. This compromises the conservation of social legacy and the passing down of customary information to more youthful ages.

5. **Influence on Worldwide Environment:**
The Icy assumes a pivotal part in the worldwide environment framework. As it warms and ice softens, it influences the dissemination examples of the climate and sea, affecting weather conditions all over the planet. A portion of the worldwide outcomes include:

Disturbance of the Fly Stream: Changes in the Icy can adjust the way of behaving of the fly stream, prompting more steady and outrageous weather conditions in mid-scope areas, including heatwaves, cold spells, and delayed times of downpour or dry season.

Worldwide Criticism Circles: The arrival of ozone depleting substances from defrosting permafrost and changes in albedo (reflectivity) because of less ice cover make criticism circles that speed up a dangerous atmospheric devation.

Sea Course: Changes in the Icy can disturb the Atlantic Meridional Upsetting Dissemination (AMOC), a vital part of worldwide sea flow. This can have expansive consequences for local environments and ocean levels.

6. **Monetary Effects:**

Environmental change in the Icy is opening up new monetary open doors and difficulties. As the ice softens, already distant regions become accessible for asset extraction, transportation, and the travel industry. This presents both monetary potential and ecological dangers, for example, oil slicks and the interruption of neighborhood environments.

7. **Security Concerns:**

The changing Cold scene raises security worries, as dissolving ice opens up new courses for delivery and asset investigation. This can prompt international pressures and expanded military presence in the district.

Relief and Variation:

Tending to the effects of environmental change in the Icy requires a two-crease approach:

Moderation: Endeavors to decrease ozone depleting substance outflows universally are crucial for slow the pace of Cold warming. Peaceful accords like the Paris Arrangement mean to restrict worldwide temperature increments and relieve the impacts of environmental change.

Variation: Icy people group and countries should adjust to the progressions currently in progress. This incorporates building strong framework, creating maintainable practices, and teaming up to address shared difficulties.

2

Chapter 2

Arctic Lullabies

Cold Bedtime songs isn't simply a title; it is an entryway to a universe of music, culture, and nature that catches the quintessence of the Icy. This melodic excursion takes us through the frozen scenes and strong networks of the far north, offering us an exceptional viewpoint on life in quite possibly of the most remote and outrageous climate on The planet. As we investigate the idea of "Icy Bedtime songs," we will dive into the entrancing mix of craftsmanship and culture that describes the Cold locale and find how it fills in as a wellspring of motivation, association, and strength for its occupants.

The Cold: A Universe of Limits

The Cold, arranged at the northernmost piece of our planet, is known for its cruel environment, distinct scenes, and exceptional excellence. This area includes the Icy Sea and the encompassing terrains of The Frozen North, Canada, Greenland, Scandinavia, and Russia. With its cold temperatures, huge ice fields, and novel environments, the Icy stands as a position of noteworthy differentiation.

The outrageous environment of the Cold isn't simply a test; it is a lifestyle for individuals who call this district home. Possessing where temperatures can decrease to - 40°C (- 40°F) or lower, where the sun vanishes for quite a long time during the Polar Evening, and where permafrost stretches out for meters underneath the ground requires flexibility, versatility, and a profound association with the land.

Cold Societies: A Rich Embroidery

The Cold isn't simply a frozen wild; it's a locale possessed by a rich embroidery of societies. Native people groups, including the Inuit, Saami, and Yupik, have lived together as one with the Cold climate for ages. Their societies are profoundly interlaced with the land, the ocean, and the rhythms of nature.

These societies have created special customs, dialects, and lifestyles that are firmly associated with the climate. From conventional hunting and fishing practices to narrating and the making of workmanship, the native people groups of the Icy have kept a profound bond with the land and ocean.

Music as an Outflow of Icy Culture

Music assumes a focal part in Cold culture. It fills in for the purpose of correspondence, a vessel for narrating, and a method for associating with the past. The Cold's melodic practices are assorted and well established in the scene and the normal world.

These melodic articulations have been gone down through ages and keep on flourishing in the Cold people group.

Throat Singing (Inuit): In the Canadian Cold, Inuit ladies practice throat singing, a work of art that mirrors the hints of nature and regular day to day existence. It frequently includes two ladies standing eye to eye and alternating delivering a progression of sounds, making a musical and hypnotizing execution.

Joik (Saami): The Saami nation of northern Scandinavia have a one of a kind type of singing known as joik. Joiks are private and intelligent melodies that commend people, creatures, or spots. Each joik is a profoundly close to home and melodic articulation of the subject.

Drum Moving (Yupik and Inuit): Drum moving is a fundamental piece of the Yupik and Inuit societies in The Frozen North. It includes the utilization of drums produced using creature skins and the musical and celebratory exhibition of conventional tunes and moves.

Cold Bedtime songs: A Melodic Excursion

The expression "Icy Bedtime songs" catches the pith of Cold music, especially the delicate and calming tunes that inspire the soul of the locale. These children's songs fill various needs in Cold culture:

Mitigating and Holding: Cold bedtime songs are utilized to quiet babies and make major areas of strength for an among guardians and kids. They offer solace and consolation in a difficult climate.

Associating with Nature: Numerous Cold cradlesongs integrate the hints of the normal world, from the murmuring of the breeze to the delicate lapping of waves on the shore. These components interface the audience to the climate and its excellence.

Narrating: Bedtime songs are a type of narrating in Icy culture. They convey conventional information, describe legends, and pass down social legacy starting with one age then onto the next.

Conventional Instruments:

Notwithstanding vocal music, the Cold flaunts different conventional instruments that are basic to the locale's melodic practices:

The Drum: Drums, frequently produced using creature stows away, are generally utilized in Icy music. They give the cadenced establishment to tunes and moves, with the reverberation of the drum mirroring the power and magnificence of the land.

The Jaw Harp: The jaw harp, produced using a slight piece of metal or bone, is an unmistakable instrument in the Saami culture. Its twanging sound is suggestive of the Icy scene.

The Drumstick: Cut from wood or bone, drumsticks are utilized to strike the drum's surface, making a cadenced beat that goes with singing and moving.

Contemporary Articulations:

While conventional music stays a fundamental piece of Cold culture, contemporary Icy performers are additionally investigating new types and styles, combining current impacts with their rich melodic legacy. These performers are tracking down creative ways of conveying the exceptional magnificence and difficulties of life in the Icy to a worldwide crowd.

Natural Topics:

Environmental change is influencing the Cold at a disturbing rate. Accordingly, numerous Cold artists are integrating ecological subjects into their music, bringing issues to light about the difficulties looked by the locale and its occupants. They utilize their music as a stage to feature the significance of protecting the Cold and relieving the effects of environmental change.

Worldwide Coordinated effort:

Cold performers frequently work together with craftsmen from around the world, making a worldwide melodic discourse that rises above lines and limits. These coordinated efforts act as a demonstration of the all inclusive force of music to interface individuals and convey feelings and thoughts.

2.1 Introduction to Polar Wildlife Lullabies

The polar districts, situated at the outrageous finishes of our planet, are home to the absolute most interesting and enrapturing untamed life on The planet. The Cold and Antarctic are portrayed by their bone chilling temperatures, shocking scenes, and a wide exhibit of tough and intriguing creatures.

These areas overflow with life, from glorious polar bears and spry penguins to marine vertebrates and birds adjusted to the most extreme circumstances. In the accompanying investigation, we will present the idea of "Polar Untamed life Bedtime songs" and dive into the universe of these momentous animals, their living spaces, and the melodic and social accounts that commend their reality.

The Polar Areas: Cold and Antarctic

The polar areas comprise of the Cold and the Antarctic, each with its particular qualities, geology, and natural life.

Cold:

The Cold is the northernmost polar district, enveloping the Icy Sea and the encompassing grounds of Gold country, Canada, Greenland, Scandinavia, and Russia. It is an area of ocean ice, permafrost, tundra, and interesting environments. The Cold is known for its polar bears, seals, whales, and a variety of bird species.

Antarctic:

The Antarctic, then again, is the southernmost polar locale and is basically made out of a huge ice sheet covering the mainland. It is the domain of penguins, seals, gooney birds, and different seabirds. While the Icy is basically a sea encircled via land, the Antarctic is the inverse, with a tremendous mainland encompassed by sea.

Both polar areas experience outrageous cold, with temperatures that can fall to - 40°C (- 40°F) or lower. Notwithstanding their cold scenes, these districts have one of a kind environments that have adjusted to the difficult circumstances.

Polar Natural life: One of a kind Variations

Polar untamed life has developed momentous transformations to flourish in the outrageous conditions of the Cold and Antarctic. These variations include:

Thick Protection: Numerous creatures in polar districts have thick layers of fat or fur to protect themselves from the virus. For instance, seals and walruses have lard, while polar bears have thick fur and a thick layer of fat.

Countercurrent Intensity Trade: Certain species have particular veins that permit them to moderate body heat. For instance, penguins have veins in their flippers that limit heat misfortune.

Disguise: Icy creatures, like the Icy fox, have created white fur to mix in with the blanketed scene, while Antarctic creatures like the Adélie penguin have dark backs and white stomaches for submerged cover.

Specific Eating regimens: Numerous polar creatures have adjusted to their current circumstance by having particular weight control plans. For example, the polar bear is a carnivore that essentially benefits from seals, while penguins are talented trackers of fish and krill.

Rearing and Mating Methodologies: Icy and Antarctic species have created novel conceptive systems. Head penguins, for instance, hatch their eggs on their feet, while seals conceive an offspring on ocean ice.

Difficulties to Polar Untamed life

Polar untamed life faces various difficulties, essentially determined by environmental change and human exercises. These difficulties include:

Liquefying Ocean Ice: The softening of ocean ice in the Cold and the Antarctic effects the territory and hunting grounds of species like polar bears and seals.

Loss of Prey: Changes in the circulation and wealth of prey species because of warming waters and living space debasement represent a danger to animal groups like penguins and seabirds.

Contamination: Contamination, including plastics and synthetics, influences polar creatures' wellbeing and their biological systems.

Overfishing: Business fishing represents a danger to the sensitive equilibrium of marine pecking orders in the polar locales.

The travel industry Effect: The travel industry in polar areas, while giving financial open doors, can likewise upset natural life and their territories while possibly not appropriately made due.

The Idea of Polar Natural life Children's songs

Polar Untamed life Bedtime songs, as an idea, addresses the amicable transaction of music, culture, and the regular world. This idea recognizes that music has the ability to interface people with the extraordinary and delicate environments of the Icy and Antarctic, filling in as a scaffold among individuals and the untamed life that possess these polar scenes. The expression "bedtime songs" accentuates the significance of sustaining and saving these locales for the future, featuring the delicate equilibrium of the polar environments.

Melodic Accounts in Polar Natural life Cradlesongs

Music has forever been a useful asset for conveying feelings, stories, and social legacy. With regards to the polar areas, melodic stories fill a few needs:

Social Protection: Native people group in the Cold and Antarctic have rich melodic practices that pass down their social legacy. These melodic stories commend the climate, creatures, and the association among people and nature.

Natural Mindfulness: Performers from around the world utilize their specialty to bring issues to light about the moves looked by polar untamed life because of environmental change and human exercises. Their tunes frequently convey a message of preservation and ecological stewardship.

Festivity of Untamed life: Polar natural life children's songs commend the greatness of the creatures that call these locales home. Melodies and sytheses honor polar bears, penguins, seals, and the many bird species that characterize the polar scenes.

Native and Social Importance

The native people groups of the Cold and Antarctic, like the Inuit, Saami, Yupik, and native gatherings of the Antarctic, have a significant association with the natural life and the terrains they possess. Their social importance is reflected in their customary melodies, moves, and creative articulations that honor the climate and its occupants.

The Force of Joint effort

Performers and specialists from around the world frequently team up with native networks in the polar areas to make music that rises above lines and societies. These joint efforts praise the variety and versatility of polar untamed life and stress the significance of saving these delicate environments.

Environmental Change and Protection Topics

Environmental change is an always present subject in polar untamed life cradlesongs. Performers utilize their foundation to cause to notice the fast changes happening in these districts and the requirement for worldwide activity to battle environmental change. These tunes frequently rouse people to do whatever it may take to safeguard the polar climate and its exceptional occupants.

Contemporary Articulations and Developments

While conventional music stays a vital piece of polar culture, contemporary craftsmen are investigating new kinds and styles to communicate the excellence and difficulties of life in the Cold and Antarctic. These performers are tracking down inventive ways of conveying the substance of these districts and their natural life to a worldwide crowd.

2.2 The Role of Lullabies in Nature

Bedtime songs are widespread articulations of affection, solace, and consolation, sung to alleviate babies and youngsters to rest. These delicate, melodic tunes have been gone down through ages, giving a common social and close to home association. While bedtime songs are normally connected with human consideration for babies, the mitigating characteristics of music stretch out past the support. In the normal world, bedtime songs take on an alternate structure, serving fundamental jobs in different biological systems. In this investigation, we will dive into the job of bedtime songs in nature and how they add to the prosperity and endurance of various species.

1. **Correspondence and Holding:**

In the animals of the world collectively, numerous species use sounds and melodies to convey and bond inside their gatherings. These vocalizations can be considered cradlesongs from a more extensive perspective, as they make a feeling of association, wellbeing, and commonality among bunch individuals.

1. **Birds:**
   Birds are notable for their vocalizations, which assume critical parts in their lives. Birdsong isn't just a method for laying an out area, draw in mates, and caution of hunters yet in addition a type of holding inside a herd. Some bird species sing calming melodies to their chicks, upgrading the parent-posterity bond and giving a feeling that all is well with the world.
2. **Whales and Dolphins:**

Marine well evolved creatures like whales and dolphins are exceptionally friendly creatures. They utilize complex vocalizations, frequently alluded to as "melodies," to speak with each other. These tunes support bunch attachment and family bonds, similar as the cradlesongs that guardians sing to their human youngsters.

2. Natural Mindfulness:

A few creatures use vocalizations, similar to children's songs, to stay caution to changes in their current circumstance. These sounds assist them with remaining cautious and receptive to possible dangers and open doors.

1. **Frogs and Amphibians:**
   Creatures of land and water, for example, frogs and frogs produce a wide assortment of vocalizations, including "ad calls" to draw in mates and "caution calls" to caution others of risk. The last option can be viewed as children's songs as in they effectively quiet individual creatures of land and water and alarm them to hunters.

2. **Bugs:**

Bug species like crickets and cicadas produce melodies to draw in mates, a lay out area, or direction inside a gathering. These melodies capability as a sort of cradlesong, permitting bugs to convey and stay in a state of harmony with their environmental elements.

3. Sustaining and Calming:

In the animals of the world collectively, the demonstration of really focusing on and alleviating posterity is a fundamental part of parental way of behaving. While not equivalent to the human custom of singing children's songs, this sustaining conduct satisfies a comparable job.

1. **Elephants:**
   Elephants are profoundly friendly and keen animals. Moms and other relatives frequently take part in delicate vocalizations and actual contact to comfort and alleviate youthful elephants. These

demonstrations of care should be visible as what could be compared to cradlesongs in the normal world.

2. Primates:

Primate species like chimpanzees and gorillas show maternal ways of behaving like human bedtime songs. Moms use vocalizations and actual touch to quiet and bond with their posterity, building up family associations.

4. Cautioning Signs:

In nature, cradlesongs can likewise appear as advance notice flags that ready others to expected risks, empowering a planned reaction for the wellbeing of the gathering.

1. Birds:

Birds utilize different vocalizations to flag the presence of hunters or different dangers. These caution calls capability as a type of cradlesong, giving an admonition to different individuals from the gathering and empowering them to look for wellbeing.

2. Grassland Canines:

Grassland canines are known for their multifaceted correspondence framework, which incorporates cautioning calls. At the point when one grassland canine identifies a hunter, it discharges a particular caution call, making others aware of seek shelter. These calls can be viewed as a type of cradlesong, effectively safeguarding the local area.

5. Natural Congruity:

In nature, bedtime songs, as creature vocalizations, add to the general congruity and equilibrium of environments. These sounds have developed as a component of the unpredictable snare of life, guaranteeing that species coincide and adjust to their environmental elements.

1. Timberland Biological systems:

In timberland biological systems, birdsongs make a mitigating setting to life in the forest. The songs of woodland birds are superb to the human ear as well as assume an imperative part in keeping up with the biological equilibrium. Birds scatter seeds, control bug populaces, and assist with pollinating plants, adding to a sound and different timberland.

2. **Coral Reefs:**

Coral reefs are lively submerged environments where fish and marine life rely upon a perplexing arrangement of sounds and correspondence. The sounds delivered by fish and other reef occupants add to the general wellbeing and strength of these fragile conditions. These submerged bedtime songs help in tracking down mates, laying out domains, and advance notice of risk.

3. **Meadows:**

In meadow environments, the calls of grassland canines and different creatures assist with keeping up with equilibrium and collaboration among various species. These sounds act as a type of cradlesong that keeps the meadows flourishing and takes into consideration the conjunction of different creatures.

2.3 Understanding Arctic Animal Behavior

The Cold, a tremendous and outrageous climate, is home to a wide exhibit of novel and versatile creature species. Understanding Cold creature conduct is fundamental for logical examination as well as for protection endeavors and the safeguarding of these amazing environments. In the accompanying investigation, we will dig into the complexities of Cold creature conduct, the transformations that empower them to flourish in unforgiving circumstances, and the difficulties they face in an evolving environment.

1. **Endurance in Outrageous Circumstances:**

Cold creatures have developed a scope of variations to flourish in the difficult states of their current circumstance. The most clear test is the super cold, with temperatures that can drop to - 40°C

(- 40°F) or lower. A few key variations include:

Thick Protection: Numerous Icy creatures, like polar bears and seals, have grown thick layers of fat and fur to give protection from the cold and hold body heat.

Countercurrent Intensity Trade: A few creatures, similar to penguins, have specific circulatory frameworks that permit them to keep heat misfortune from their furthest points, keeping imperative organs warm.

Cover: Cold foxes and ptarmigans change the shade of their fur or plumes with the seasons, adjusting to the white snow in winter and the earthy colored tundra in summer to stay away from hunters and help in hunting.

Specific Eating regimens: The brutal states of as far as possible the accessibility of food. Numerous Icy creatures, like polar bears and seals, are predatory and depend on hunting seals and fish for food.

2. **Occasional Movement and Rearing:**

Cold creatures are exceptionally sensitive to the occasional changes that influence their current circumstance. They have adjusted their ways of behaving to make the most of the restricted glimpses of daylight for taking care of, reproducing, and raising youthful. Key ways of behaving include:

Occasional Movement: Numerous types of birds, for example, the snow goose and Cold tern, relocate large number of kilometers between their Icy favorable places and wintering regions in milder environments. This relocation guarantees admittance to plentiful food and ideal reproducing conditions.

Rearing and Parental Consideration: Cold creatures normally time their reproducing seasons to concur with the concise Icy summer when food is all the more promptly accessible. Subsequent to conceiving an offspring, creatures like harp seals and reindeer give extraordinary parental consideration to guarantee the endurance of their posterity in cruel circumstances.

3. **Social Way of behaving and Variations:**

Icy creatures frequently show social ways of behaving that improve their endurance in the brutal climate. These ways of behaving assist them with tracking down food, share warmth, and give assurance against hunters. A few models include:

Clustering and Gathering: Numerous Icy birds and vertebrates group together for warmth. Sovereign penguins, for example, accumulate in enormous gatherings to cluster and hatch their eggs during the brutal Antarctic winter.

Agreeable Hunting: A few animal varieties, similar to wolves and Cold foxes, chase in packs, coordinating to bring down bigger prey. This methodology permits them to get to adequate food assets and increment their possibilities of endurance.

Social Bonds: The perplexing social designs of creatures like polar bears and elephants help in sharing information about food sources and offer help for youthful creatures during the growing experience.

4. **Regenerative Methodologies:**

In the Cold, where food can be scant, creatures frequently show extraordinary regenerative systems. These systems permit them to deliver and really focus on posterity while limiting the effect on their capacity to make due in brutal circumstances. Key transformations include:

Defer in Implantation: A few creatures, similar to the Cold ground squirrel, show a postponed implantation technique. They mate not long after arising out of hibernation, however the prepared eggs don't embed in that frame of mind until the ecological circumstances are better.

Polygamy and Romance Shows: Certain species, like polar bears and seals, participate in polygamous reproducing frameworks. Guys might participate in intricate romance presentations to seek females.

Birth Timing: Cold creatures, for example, reindeer, time their births to harmonize with the beginning of the developing season, furnishing youthful creatures with admittance to bountiful food.

5. **Challenges in an Evolving Environment:**

The Cold is encountering the impacts of environmental change at a sped up rate. As temperatures increase and ocean ice softens, Icy creature conduct is being upset. The difficulties they face include:

Loss of Territory: The softening of ocean ice influences the natural surroundings of species like polar bears and seals, making it more trying for these creatures to chase and raise.

Changes in Food Accessibility: Changes in the circulation and wealth of prey species because of warming waters and natural surroundings debasement represent a danger to animal types like polar bears and marine vertebrates.

Ecological Pressure: Changes in temperature and atmospheric conditions can actuate pressure in Cold creatures, affecting their wellbeing and conceptive achievement.

Human Aggravation: Expanded human movement in the Icy, including transportation and the travel industry, can disturb creature ways of behaving and territories.

2.4 The Connection Between Animal Sounds and Lullabies

Cradlesongs have been a widespread part of human culture for a really long time, filling in as relieving, melodic articulations of adoration, care, and solace. These delicate tunes are frequently connected with sleep time and are utilized to hush babies and kids to rest. Strangely, there is an interesting and significant association among cradlesongs and the hints of the normal world, especially the sounds created by creatures. This association, however not generally promptly obvious, features the interchange between human culture and the climate. In this investigation, we will dive into the association between creature sounds and cradlesongs, analyzing what nature's tunes have roused and meant for these ageless melodies.

1. **The All inclusiveness of Children's songs:**
   Bedtime songs are a widespread peculiarity. They exist in societies across the globe, rising above topographical, etymological, and social limits. These tunes share normal attributes, including delicate songs, delicate rhythms, and dreary examples. This all inclusiveness addresses the basic human sense to support and solace the youthful, as well as the craving to interface with the normal world.

2. **Nature as the Wellspring of Motivation:**

Human societies have for some time been enlivened by their general surroundings, drawing upon the sounds and rhythms of nature to make music and craftsmanship. The association among children's songs and creature sounds mirrors the well established connection among people and the climate. Over the entire course of time, individuals have integrated components of nature into their imaginative articulations, including cradlesongs. The accompanying models represent this association:

1. **Birds as Melodic Motivations:**
   Birdsong is a wellspring of motivation for some cradlesongs. The pleasant and quieting tunes of birds have affected human music for a really long time. In many societies, bird tunes are integrated into cradlesongs, making an environment of quietness and association with nature. These cradlesongs frequently copy the tunes of explicit bird species, like songbirds, canaries, or larks.

2. **Water as a Mitigating Component:**

The sound of streaming water, whether from a prattling creek or sea waves, is one more wellspring of motivation for bedtime songs. The cadenced and relieving characteristics of water sounds are frequently integrated into melodies to make a serene feeling, hushing youngsters to rest. The redundancy and consistency of these sounds impersonate the consoling idea of bedtime songs.

3. Social Varieties:

Cradlesongs, enlivened by creature sounds and the regular world, change across societies. These varieties are an impression of the different conditions and environments wherein various societies have created. The selection of creatures and normal components in children's songs can be profoundly representative and socially huge:

1. **Local American Bedtime songs:**

   Numerous Local American bedtime songs integrate creature references, like the hoot of an owl or the call of a coyote. These creatures hold social and profound importance for native people groups. The cradlesongs interface kids to the creatures of their current circumstance and impart a feeling of congruity with the normal world.

2. **African Cradlesongs:**

African cradlesongs frequently incorporate references to creatures local to the area, like lions, elephants, or birds. These bedtime songs convey a feeling of security and association with the creatures that coincide with networks in Africa.

4. The Job of Creative mind:

Bedtime songs that consolidate creature sounds frequently connect with the youngster's creative mind. By summoning the sounds and rhythms of the normal world, these cradlesongs make a tactile encounter that transports kids to a tranquil and agreeable domain. The innovative components of these tunes impart a feeling of marvel and interest in the climate.

5. Creature Sounds as Similitudes:

In certain cradlesongs, creature sounds are utilized allegorically to convey more profound implications. Creature conduct and vocalizations might represent characteristics or excellencies that guardians wish to impart in their kids. For instance, a cradlesong that references the strength of a lion might urge a youngster to be valiant and certain.

6. Loosening up Soundscapes:

Notwithstanding cradlesongs propelled by creature sounds, there are structures that imitate the more extensive soundscapes of nature. These may incorporate stirring leaves, delicate breezes, or the delicate patter of downpour. These bedtime songs mean to make a climate of peacefulness and unwinding, much the same as the quieting hints of the regular world.

7. Present day Understandings:

While customary cradlesongs frequently consolidate creature sounds, current understandings of these melodies keep on drawing from the hints of the climate. Contemporary specialists have mixed electronic sounds, recorded nature sounds, and customary melodic components to make bedtime songs that mirror the intricacies of the cutting edge world. These sytheses offer a combination of innovation and nature, bringing the relieving characteristics of the outside into the computerized age.

8. Past Cradlesongs: Natural Soundscapes:

The association between creature sounds and cradlesongs stretches out past these sleep time tunes. The field of "ecological soundscapes" has arisen, zeroing in on the recording and safeguarding of the hints of nature. These soundscapes catch the orchestra of the regular world, including creature calls, wind stirring through trees, and the delicate mumble of streams. These accounts serve as imaginative articulations as well as significant apparatuses for logical examination and protection endeavors.

Chapter 3

The Walrus's Whisper

Quite a long time ago, in the frigid domains of the Cold, there carried on with a savvy and old walrus named Olna. He was known to the animals of the North as the manager of significant insight and the watchman of the Icy's mysteries. Olna's heart was essentially as huge as the Cold Sea, and his tusks, cleaned by endless long periods of shimmering in the northern sun, were a demonstration of the immortal information he held. Olna's story, "The Walrus' Murmur," was an account passed down from one age to another, loved by walruses as well as by polar bears, seals, and every one of the animals of the frozen wild. It was an account of marvel and illumination, of the interconnectedness of life in the Cold, and the significant examples it held.

The Call of the Northern Breezes

The story started with the call of the northern breezes. In the core of the Icy, there was a spot known as the "Murmuring Ice," a locale where ice shelves mumbled and ice sheets sang. It was said that assuming one listened cautiously, they could hear the privileged insights of the Cold murmured by the actual ice. Olna, with his profound and knowing eyes, frequently withdrew to the Murmuring Ice to pay attention to the insight conveyed by the breezes.

The Murmuring Ice was a position of reflection, where the walls of old ice sheets held accounts of when the world was cold and unforgiving. The frozen scene was not vacant yet overflowing with life. Olna, with a gathering of walrus mates, would accumulate on the ice to pay attention to the mumbles of the ice sheets.

The Account of the Ice Bear

At some point, while they paid attention to the ice, Olna started to tell a story that had been murmured to him by the breezes. It was the narrative of the "Ice Bear," an incredible polar bear whose fur was pretty much as white as the snow, and whose heart was basically as immense as the Icy Sea.

The Ice Bear was known for his solidarity and boldness, however he likewise had a delicacy that filled the hearts of the people who crossed his way. He meandered the frosty wild, not as a savage hunter, but rather as a gatekeeper of the land and its animals. He would assist the seals with finding their breathing openings and offer his glow with youthful fledglings who had lost themselves. The Ice Bear grasped the fragile equilibrium of life in the Cold and promised to safeguard it.

The Tune of the Seals

In the following part of the story, Olna described the "Tune of the Seals." The marks of the Icy had a melody that reverberated through the frozen waters. Their voices, however tormenting, were a demonstration of their flexibility and versatility.

The seals had for some time been the prey of the polar bears and the orca whales, however they had additionally taken in the specialty of endurance. Their tunes, reverberating through the ice, told stories of the moving flows, the rhythms of the tides, and the insider facts of the submerged world. They passed down their tunes from one age to another, guaranteeing that the insight of the seals would persevere.

The Dance of Aurora Borealis

Perhaps of the most charming part in Olna's story was "The Dance of Aurora Borealis." The Cold evenings were in many cases enlightened by the aurora borealis, a stunning showcase of varieties that painted the night sky. To the animals of the North, these divine lights were a wellspring of marvel and motivation.

The walruses, seals, and polar bears would accumulate underneath the moving lights, looking up in wonder. They accepted that Aurora Borealis were the spirits of their progenitors, sharing their insight and favors. Olna instructed that the dance of Aurora Borealis was a sign of the interconnectedness of all life in the Icy and the significance of safeguarding their frozen home.

The Illustration of the Dissolving Ice

As Olna's story proceeded, the story took a dismal turn. The ice of the Cold was softening, and the animals of the North confronted a dubious future. The walrus shared an example from the liquefying ice: the significance of transformation and collaboration.

Despite an evolving environment, the Cold creatures expected to co-operate to track down better approaches to get by. The dissolving ice was an obvious update that the difficulties they confronted were not of their making, but rather still up in the air to confront them with versatility and solidarity.

The Tradition of the Murmur

The last section of Olna's story was "The Tradition of the Murmur." Olna underscored the significance of passing down the insight of the Icy to the future. He trusted that the creatures of the North held the keys to a manageable future, and that their accounts and information ought to be valued and safeguarded.

The tradition of the Murmur was a source of inspiration, an update that the animals of the Icy were in good company in their battles. Individuals from all edges of the world expected to comprehend and uphold the protection of the Cold and its occupants.

3.1 Introduction to the Walrus

The walrus, a momentous and charming marine warm blooded creature, holds a unique spot in the hearts and societies of the people who stay in or concentrate on the Icy locales. These unmistakable animals, with their conspicuous tusks and huge, blubbery bodies, are symbols of the frozen north as well as fundamental players in the Icy biological system. In this investigation, we will dig into the universe of the walrus, looking at their science, conduct, social importance, and the difficulties they face in a quickly evolving climate.

1. **Scientific categorization and Order**

   To comprehend the walrus, we should start with its scientific categorization and order. The walrus, deductively known as Odobenus rosmarus, has a place with the family Odobenidae and is the sole enduring individual from this family. There are two perceived subspecies of walrus: the Atlantic walrus (Odobenus rosmarus) and the Pacific walrus (Odobenus rosmarus divergens). These subspecies vary somewhat in actual attributes and topographical conveyance, with the Atlantic walrus possessing the eastern side of the Cold Sea and the Pacific walrus dwelling along the western side, including the Bering Ocean.

2. **Actual Qualities**

   Walruses are hitting animals with a few remarkable actual highlights. Their most notable attribute is without a doubt their long, ivory tusks, which can grow up to 3 feet long in guys and fairly more limited in females. These tusks are lengthened canine teeth and fill various needs, for example, helping with pulling themselves out of the water and making breathing openings in the ocean ice.

   The walrus' skin is thick and badly crumpled, fundamentally to give protection in the bone chilling Icy waters. Their fat layer under the skin directs their internal heat level and gives lightness. Grown-up walruses can weigh somewhere in the range of 1,500 to 3,000 pounds, with guys for the most part being bigger and heavier than females. Their expansive, flipper-like front appendages permit them to swim and explore proficiently in the sea.

One of the most charming parts of a walrus' appearance is its bristles, known as vibrissae. These bristles are unbelievably touchy and assist the creature with recognizing prey in the dim profundities of the Icy ocean, as well as find shellfish and other food sources covered in the sea depths.

3. **Territory and Dispersion**

Walruses are exceptionally adjusted to their super Icy climate. They are normally found in the shallow mainland racks of the Icy Sea, as well as in the Bering Ocean. These regions give sufficient chances to walruses to benefit from their favored eating routine of benthic spineless creatures, like shellfishes, mussels, and snails.

Throughout the mid year months, walruses will generally possess areas of drifting ocean ice, where they use it as a stage to rest, mingle, and bring forth their young. In the colder time of year, they frequently move to more steady ice floes.

Their dissemination changes via season, with the Pacific walrus for the most part living nearer to the edge of the ice, while the Atlantic walrus favors denser pack ice.

4. **Conduct and Social Design**

Walruses are known for their gregarious nature and can frequently be tracked down in huge gatherings, known as haulouts. These get-togethers serve a few capabilities, for example, security from hunters like polar bears and mingling. Walruses are profoundly vocal, utilizing different sounds like snaps and chime like whistles to convey inside their gatherings.

The social construction of a walrus haulout is perplexing, with predominant guys laying out regions and vieing for admittance to females during the reproducing season. Females will generally be more friendly, frequently shaping affectionate bonds and really focusing on their young together. Little guys, brought into the world on the ice in the spring, are profoundly reliant upon their moms and are breast fed for around two years.

5. **Diet and Taking care of Conduct**

Walruses are principally predatory and feed on a tight eating routine of benthic spineless creatures, especially bivalves like mollusks and mussels. They utilize their vibrissae to identify go after the sea floor, and their tusks are fundamental apparatuses for digging and tearing open shells.

Their taking care of conduct is a wonder of variation to their current circumstance. Walruses are fit for plunging to amazing profundities, frequently arriving at up to 300 feet or more. They can remain lowered for expanded periods, on account of their proficient oxygen stockpiling and flow frameworks. During a solitary plunge, they might consume many shellfishes, making them fundamental supporters of the Cold environment.

6. **Social Importance**

The walrus holds a critical spot in the way of life of Icy native people groups. For a really long time, walrus meat, lard, skin, and bones have been fundamental for the endurance of these networks, giving a rich wellspring of food, dress, and devices. The tusks, specifically, are exceptionally valued for their adaptability, filling in as the natural substance for different imaginative and utilitarian things, including ivory carvings, apparatuses, and hunting weapons.

The emblematic meaning of the walrus goes past its reasonable worth. It is in many cases highlighted in Cold fables and folklore, with stories and legends commending the walrus' solidarity, flexibility, and versatility in the brutal northern climate. These stories mirror the profound social association between native people groups and the walrus.

7. **Protection and Dangers**

Likewise with numerous Icy species, walruses face critical difficulties notwithstanding environmental change. The continuous warming of the Cold has prompted the deficiency of ocean ice, which fills in as basic living space for these marine well evolved creatures. The retreating ice has constrained walruses to pull out ashore in certain areas, prompting packing, expanded pressure, and higher death rates, especially among calves.

One more critical danger to walruses is business hunting. Albeit global guidelines and preservation endeavors have prompted limitations on walrus hunting, unlawful hunting actually happens in certain areas. Progressives and scientists are working industriously to screen and safeguard these famous animals.

3.2 The Sounds of Walrus

The walrus, known for its unmistakable appearance and entrancing way of behaving, isn't just a visual wonder yet in addition a hearable miracle in the huge Icy soundscape. These marine warm blooded creatures, frequently tracked down in huge, parties, have a complicated arrangement of vocalizations and sounds that fill different needs, from correspondence inside their gatherings to route and endurance in their frigid territory. In this investigation, we will jump into the universe of the hints of the walrus, unwinding the secrets of their correspondence, echolocation, and the job these vocalizations play in their day to day routines.

1. **Correspondence Inside Haulouts**

   Walruses are profoundly friendly creatures, frequently congregating in huge gatherings called haulouts. These get-togethers serve different capabilities, from giving assurance against hunters to working with social collaborations. Inside these haulouts, walruses participate in a large number of vocalizations to speak with each other.

   Snaps and Whistles: Walruses produce a progression of snaps and chime like whistles that act as a type of social correspondence.

These sounds can be heard above and underneath water, making them fundamental for planning bunch exercises and keeping up with social securities.

Calls and Vocalizations: Walruses likewise settle on various decisions and vocalizations that show their close to home state and pass on data about their expectations. For example, during connections between guys seeking females during the rearing season, forceful calls can be heard. Moms and calves have particular calls that assist them with perceiving each other in swarmed haulouts.

2. **Rearing Calls and Conceptive Correspondence**

   During the rearing season, male walruses vie for admittance to females, and vocalizations assume a urgent part in this cycle.

   Thundering and Howling: Predominant guys frequently produce clearly and low-recurrence thunders and roars to affirm their presence and strength. These vocalizations act as an advance notice to equal guys and assist with laying out domains inside the haulout.

   Romance Calls: rather than the forceful calls, guys additionally take part in romance calls to draw in females. These calls are milder, with additional cadenced examples, and assume an essential part in charming possible mates.

3. **Mother-Calf Correspondence**

   Mother-calf correspondence is pivotal for the endurance of walrus calves, as it assists them with perceiving their moms and keep up with vicinity in swarmed haulouts.

   Unmistakable Calls: Each mother and calf have extraordinary vocalizations that permit them to recognize one another. These calls are fundamental for a calf to find its mom in an ocean of blubbery bodies and lay out a security.

   Consoling Sounds: Mother walruses produce soothing vocalizations that console their calves, assisting them with exploring the clamoring haulouts and keep away from trouble.

4. Reverberation Area and Searching

While walruses are not known for their echolocation capacities to the degree of dolphins and whales, they in all actuality do utilize sound to find their food sources.

Vibrissae and Sound Location: Walruses have profoundly delicate vibrissae (bristles) that they use to identify prey concealed in the residue on the sea floor. They produce vibrations by moving their vibrissae through the substrate and pay attention to the reverberations to find potential food sources.

Tusk Snaps: The walrus' tusks, notwithstanding their part in digging and tearing open shells, can likewise create clicking sounds when they come into contact with hard items. These snaps can help walruses recognize the construction and thickness of articles they experience, helping them in chasing after prey.

5. The Soundscape of the Cold

The Icy is an interesting and dynamic acoustic climate, rich with sounds from different sources, including wind, ice, water, and other marine life. Walrus vocalizations are a vital piece of this Cold soundscape, filling in as signs and signals in this perplexing sound woven artwork.

Transformation to the Cold Soundscape: Walruses have developed to flourish in the uproarious Icy climate. Their vocalizations are intended to slice through the encompassing commotion and extend significant distances, making them compelling for correspondence in their clamoring haulouts.

Job in Route: In the immense scopes of the Icy, walrus vocalizations assume a critical part in route and tracking down their direction through the frosty waters. These sounds assist them with keeping in touch with their gatherings and find haulouts.

6. Difficulties and Protection

As the Icy climate faces quick changes because of environmental change and human exercises, the soundscape of the district is likewise being adjusted. The diminishing ocean ice and expanding human presence, including transporting traffic and asset investigation, are making disturbances the acoustic climate that walruses rely upon.

Commotion Contamination: Expanded human exercises in the Icy have presented clamor contamination that can slow down walrus correspondence and echolocation. This aggravation might possibly prompt diminished searching achievement and expanded pressure among walrus populaces.

Suggestions for Preservation: Understanding the meaning of vocalizations in walrus conduct and endurance is fundamental for their protection. Endeavors to safeguard walrus natural surroundings and lessen anthropogenic commotion contamination are indispensable to guarantee the prosperity of these striking marine vertebrates.

3.3 The Walrus's Importance in the Arctic Ecosystem

The Cold biological system is a complicated snare of related species and natural cycles, where every part assumes a basic part in keeping up with the fragile equilibrium of life in this outrageous climate. Among the numerous famous species occupying the Icy, the walrus (Odobenus rosmarus) stands apart as a cornerstone animal groups with a huge job in the biological system. This enormous marine warm blooded animal, with its striking tusks and unmistakable appearance, serves different capabilities in the Cold food web, impacts the construction of marine networks, and has social and environmental importance. In this investigation, we dig into the significance of the walrus in the Cold biological system and analyze how changes in their populaces and conduct can have extensive ramifications for the locale.

1. **Cornerstone Species in the Cold**

   A cornerstone animal types is one that generally affects its biological system comparative with its overflow or biomass. In the Icy, the walrus possesses all the necessary qualities as a cornerstone animal groups because of its exceptional taking care of conduct and its job in forming the seaside biological systems of the Cold Sea.

Predation and Prey Control: Walruses are fundamentally benthic feeders, gaining practical experience in scrounging on the sea depths for bivalves, especially mollusks and mussels. Their taking care of conduct assists control the number of inhabitants in these spineless creatures, which with canning have flowing consequences for the whole environment. By restricting the wealth of specific prey species, walruses by implication impact the populaces of their hunters.

Living space Designing: Walruses effectively change their territories. At the point when they pull out on ice floes, they make discouragements in the ice, which can gather snow and ice over the long haul. These miseries give cover and a steady stage for other Cold species, like seals, seabirds, and little fish, which use them for resting, shedding, and reproducing.

2. **Supplement Cycling**

The Cold biological system is a brutal, supplement unfortunate climate, yet walruses assume a urgent part in supplement cycling, moving fundamental components from the marine climate to the land.

Guano Testimony: When walruses pull out on seaside land, they produce huge amounts of guano (waste). This guano contains fundamental supplements, including nitrogen and phosphorus, which advance the encompassing earthbound climate. It gives an imperative wellspring of supplements for plant development in any case fruitless Cold locales.

Trophic Fountain: The statement of supplements through walrus guano can start a trophic outpouring in the environment. The expanded plant development upholds a scope of herbivores, which, thus, give food to hunters. Consequently, walruses assist with making a progression of energy and supplements from the sea to the land.

3. **Cold Environment Construction**

   Walruses likewise assume a part in molding the design of Icy biological systems through their cooperations with different species and their effect on food networks.

   Predation and Rivalry: Walruses are prey as well as hunters. They are pursued by dominant hunters like polar bears and executioner whales. By being important for the Cold food web, they assist with controlling the populaces of their prey species and impact the elements of hunter prey connections.

   Contest with Seals: Walruses and seals share normal prey, especially benthic spineless creatures. This opposition for food assets can have significant natural outcomes, with both walruses and seals impacting the circulation and wealth of their common prey.

4. **Social and Native Importance**

   The significance of the walrus in the Cold environment goes past its biological job. It is profoundly imbued in the social and conventional acts of native networks living in the Cold area.

   Means Hunting: For quite a long time, native people groups in the Cold have depended on walruses for food. The meat, fat, skin, and tusks of walruses are fundamental for their endurance, giving food, attire, instruments, and materials for workmanship and art.

   Social Symbol: The walrus holds an extraordinary spot in Cold societies, highlighting noticeably in old stories, craftsmanship, and services. It represents strength, flexibility, and versatility notwithstanding outrageous circumstances, mirroring the qualities and customs of Icy people group.

5. **Environmental Change and Protection**

   As the Icy appearances extraordinary natural changes because of environmental change, the significance of walruses in the biological system takes on new importance. Figuring out their weaknesses and preserving their living spaces is vital for the wellbeing and soundness of the whole Cold biological system.

Ice Misfortune and Haulout Destinations: Walruses are profoundly subject to the ocean ice as haulout locales, which they use for resting, conceiving an offspring, and raising their young. The deficiency of ocean ice because of increasing temperatures powers walruses to pull out ashore, where they are more defenseless against unsettling influences and predation.

Sea Fermentation: Sea fermentation, driven by expanded carbon dioxide levels, influences the accessibility and piece of shellfish, the essential food wellspring of walruses. These progressions can affect walrus taking care of propensities and their general wellbeing.

Protection Measures: Preservation endeavors are fundamental for defend walrus populaces. Worldwide guidelines limit hunting and give insurances, however the changing Icy climate presents new difficulties. Moderating environmental change and limiting human aggravations in key walrus natural surroundings are fundamental for their drawn out endurance.

6. **Ramifications of Walrus Decline**

The downfall of walrus populaces in the Icy would have significant ramifications for the whole environment.

Modified Food Networks: A diminishing in walrus numbers could disturb the equilibrium of hunter prey connections and the dissemination of benthic spineless creatures. This could prompt changes in the design of the Cold food web, influencing various species all through the environment.

Natural surroundings Changes: The shift from ocean ice haulouts to land-based haulouts because of ice misfortune might bring about congestion and expanded contest for assets. These progressions could pressure walrus populaces and effect their conceptive achievement.

Social Misfortune: The decay of walrus populaces would socially affect native networks that rely upon these creatures for their customary practices and lifestyles.

3.4 A Walrus-inspired Lullaby

In the realm of natural life, there are not many animals as enrapturing and captivating as the walrus. These huge marine well evolved creatures, known for their grand tusks and blundering beauty, occupy the bone chilling Icy and subarctic districts of our planet. However, underneath their rough appearance lies a significant wonder that has propelled writers, craftsmen, and performers for quite a long time. we will leave on an excursion to investigate the universe of the walrus and its novel effect on an enchanting and calming bedtime song. "The Melodic Murmurs of the Walrus" is a melodic creation that commends the life and soul of these striking creatures. The children's song recounts an account of the walrus, its natural surroundings, and the persevering through sorcery of the Cold, making a piece of workmanship that can move audience members to a universe of peaceful miracle and calm reflection.

1. The Cryptic Universe of the Walrus

Before we dive into the bedtime song, understanding the perplexing universe of the walrus is fundamental. These glorious animals are the biggest seals and are separated into two species, the Atlantic walrus (Odobenus rosmarus) and the Pacific walrus (Odobenus rosmarus divergens). They are impeccably adjusted to make due in the brutal states of the Icy, where they track down their home on the ice and in the cold waters.

1. Actual Attributes

Walruses are in a flash unmistakable by their long tusks, which are, truth be told, prolonged canine teeth. These tusks fill numerous needs, including scrounging for food, pulling themselves onto ice floes, and safeguard. Grown-up guys commonly have bigger and more bended tusks than females.

Their massive mass can scare, as developed guys can gauge up to 2,000 kg (4,400 lbs), while females are to some degree more modest. Their bodies are shrouded in a layer of lard that protects them from the super cold and gives lightness in the water.

2. **Territory and Conduct**

Walruses are exceptionally gregarious creatures, and they are known for framing huge, uproarious states on ice floes or rough shores. These settlements give security from hunters like polar bears and orcas and furthermore act as friendly center points for these social creatures.

They are fundamentally herbivores and feed on a careful nutritional plan of shellfishes, snails, and different spineless creatures found on the sea floor. Their stubbles, otherwise called vibrissae, are exceptionally touchy and assist them with finding food in the cloudy profundities of the Cold waters.

The universe of the walrus is set apart by a feeling of local area, with people sharing their encounters, challenges, and delights with each other. Their vocalizations, a progression of snorts, thunders, and roars, are the foundation of this mutual correspondence.

3. **Preservation Concerns**

In spite of their astounding variations to the Icy climate, walruses face various difficulties, including environmental change, natural surroundings misfortune, and hunting. As the Cold ice keeps on contracting because of climbing temperatures, walruses are compelled to come aground in ever bigger numbers, prompting packing and expanded rivalry for food. This, thusly, has brought about higher death rates among walrus populaces.

Preservation endeavors are in progress to safeguard these exceptional creatures and their weak natural surroundings. Recording and understanding their lives is a urgent move toward guaranteeing the endurance of the walrus.

II. The Making of "The Melodic Murmurs of the Walrus"

1. **The Motivation**

   Motivation for "The Melodic Murmurs of the Walrus" struck out of nowhere one fresh, Cold night. As the sunset painted the skyline with shades of pink and purple, a gathering of walruses, their huge bodies heaped on a liquefying ice floe, made a hypnotizing display. The walruses' aggregate elegance and apathetic presence in the midst of the destruction of their changing living space made a permanent imprint on my heart.

   I felt a sense of urgency to decipher the sorcery of that second into a piece of music, a bedtime song that could catch the substance of the walrus and the charm of the Icy. It would be a cradlesong to mitigate spirits and inspire the profound association among humankind and the normal world.

2. **Melodic Creation**

   "The Melodic Murmurs of the Walrus" started as a straightforward, tormenting tune that repeated the ethereal idea of the Icy scene. The initial notes, played delicately on a piano, are delicate and slow, addressing the gradual cadence of life in the Icy. The tune was created in a minor key to convey a feeling of yearning and despairing, reflecting the walrus' weakness even with ecological changes.

   The song was then set up for a little gathering, including the piano, strings, and a solitary, full French horn. The strings gave profundity and warmth, while the French horn added a component of magnificence, suggestive of the greatness of the ice-covered Cold.

3. **Verses**

"The Melodic Murmurs of the Walrus" consolidates a bunch of reminiscent verses to recount the narrative of the walrus and its cold world. The verses convey the walrus' day to day existence, its difficulties, and its flexibility, while welcoming the audience to embrace the serenity of the Icy scene.

III. The Narrating through Music

1. **The Walrus' Excursion**

"The Melodic Murmurs of the Walrus" is a bedtime song that recounts a story. It starts with the walrus' excursion through the Cold waters, with the piano delicately directing the audience into the tremendous, frosty territory. The strings and the French horn participate, reflecting the walrus' rich developments as it coasts through the bone chilling profundities.

As the music unfurls, it takes the audience to the walrus' social events on the ice floes. The group, amicable voices of the troupe address the public existence of these creatures. The songs rise and fall like the floods of the Icy Sea, making a feeling of solidarity and reason.

2. **The Cold Scene**

The children's song likewise portrays the Icy scene. The verses and the music portray the snow-shrouded spans, the moving Aurora Borealis, and the quiet magnificence that can be viewed as in the cruelest of conditions. The French horn's magnificent tones inspire the loftiness of the polar scenes, while the strings draw out the sensitive, glasslike excellence of the ice.

As the music arrives at its apex, it catches the enchantment of the Cold's always evolving light, from the delicate, pastel shades of day break to the red hot splendor of the 12 PM sun. The audience is shipped to a domain where time appears to stop, and the significant magnificence of the regular world is enlightened.

3. **The Walrus' Flexibility**

"The Melodic Murmurs of the Walrus" isn't just about magnificence and peacefulness; it likewise features the difficulties looked by the walrus in an impacting world. The music turns out to be more grave as it mirrors the misfortune the walrus should face because of the contracting ice, the deficiency of its living space, and the rising tensions of a warming planet.

However, even notwithstanding these difficulties, the children's song underscores the walrus' versatility. The tune gets back to its underlying, encouraging notes, reminding the audience that the soul of the walrus perseveres. The piece leaves the crowd with a feeling of trust, that in the event that we regard and safeguard the normal world, the wizardry of the Cold, and the delightful animals that possess it, will persevere.

IV. The Close to home Effect

1. **A Mitigating and Encouraging Experience**
"The Melodic Murmurs of the Walrus" is most importantly a children's song, planned to be calming and encouraging. Its delicate, melodic movement and the utilization of agreeable instruments make a feeling of peacefulness, welcoming the audience to relinquish pressure and track down comfort in the music.
The piece's sluggish beat and delicate elements reflect the normal rhythms of life in the Icy, where everything moves at a conscious speed. Paying attention to this children's song is much the same as being supported in the arms of the walrus, no problem at all in the core of its Icy home.

2. **An Association with Nature**
One of the essential objectives of "The Melodic Murmurs of the Walrus" is to cultivate a more profound association with nature. By submerging the audience in the Icy soundscape, the piece empowers examination and reflection on the excellence of our planet's most out of control places. It fills in as an update that we are all essential for the very worldwide biological system and that our activities significantly affect the normal world.
The music energizes sympathy for the walrus and its battle for endurance, which, thus, can rouse people to help protection endeavors and settle on decisions that benefit the climate.

3. **A Declaration of Craftsmanship and Imagination**

"The Melodic Murmurs of the Walrus" is a demonstration of the force of workmanship and imagination in conveying complex feelings and thoughts. Through the organization of this bedtime song, the excellence and delicacy of the Icy environment show some major signs of life such that words alone would never catch.

This imaginative articulation makes a way for a reality where feeling, magnificence, and understanding converge into one. It is an update that craftsmanship, in the entirety of its structures, can act as a scaffold between the human experience and the normal world.

Chapter 4

The Beluga's Ballad

The expanses of our reality are a gold mine of life, holding onto a unimaginable variety of species that have propelled stunningness and miracle for quite a long time. Among these marine animals, the beluga whale (Delphinapterus leucas) stands apart as an image of elegance, insight, and excellence. Known as the "canary of the ocean" for its melodic vocalizations, the beluga has long charmed the human creative mind. In this 4000-word paper, we will investigate the charming universe of the beluga whale and its significant impact on "The Beluga's Melody," a melodic sythesis that tries to convey the soul and wizardry of these noteworthy marine vertebrates. This orchestra of the ocean fills in as a tribute to the beluga, commending its presence, its territory, and the persevering through marvels of the sea.

1. The Mysterious Universe of the Beluga

To comprehend the making of "The Beluga's Anthem," it is vital for first value the spellbinding universe of the beluga whale. Belugas are unmistakable, medium-sized toothed whales that occupy the Cold and subarctic districts of the Northern Side of the equator. Their immaculate white hue, vocal abilities, and energetic nature make them quite possibly of the most dearest marine specie on our planet.

1. **Actual Qualities**

   Beluga whales are effectively unmistakable because of their striking white or light dim variety, which stands out pointedly from their dim, expressive eyes. This exceptional pigmentation is a transformation to their frigid living space, and it separates them from different cetaceans. Belugas are likewise known for their absence of a dorsal blade, rather including a little, bump like edge on their backs.

   These marine warm blooded animals can develop to associate with 13 to 20 feet long and regularly weigh somewhere in the range of 1,100 and 3,500 pounds. Their adjusted temples, or "melons," house echolocation organs that they use to explore and impart in the complex submerged world.

2. **Natural surroundings and Conduct**

   Beluga whales are exceptionally friendly animals, shaping very close gatherings, or cases, that can number from a couple of people to hundreds. These units assume a fundamental part in the existence of the beluga, giving security, hunting open doors, and social communications.

   One of the most intriguing parts of beluga conduct is their vocalizations. They are known for their different collection of sounds, which can go from whistles and snaps to tunes that can keep going for minutes. These vocalizations are a method for correspondence inside the unit, utilized for organizing exercises, mingling, and conceivably in any event, distinguishing people.

   Belugas are deft feeders and are known to consume a wide assortment of prey, including fish, squid, and shellfish. Their capacity to adjust to changing food sources is one of the elements adding to their endurance in the difficult Cold climate.

3. Preservation Concerns

In spite of their versatility and flexibility, beluga whales face different dangers, principally coming from human exercises. Environmental change, natural surroundings corruption, transporting traffic, and modern improvement are difficulties to beluga populaces. Moreover, belugas in certain districts are pursued for their meat, skin, and fat.

Preservation endeavors are in progress to safeguard these appealling marine well evolved creatures, underscoring the need to protect their regular territories and lessen human effects on their current circumstance. Recording and understanding their lives is significant for guaranteeing the endurance of the beluga whale.

II. The Introduction of "The Beluga's Ditty"

1. The Flash of Motivation

The beginning of "The Beluga's Song" was a snapshot of luck, a crash of workmanship and nature that lighted an imaginative flash. It occurred on a fresh Icy morning when I saw a case of beluga whales smoothly skimming through the frosty waters. Their unadulterated white structures appeared to move among the gleaming ice floes, and the reasonable, cold air was loaded up with the ethereal hints of their pleasant calls.

I was quickly struck by the significant association between these animals and their current circumstance — the sea, the ice, and the sky. Their excellence, effortlessness, and the unpleasant nature of their vocalizations addressed something profound inside my spirit. I realize that I expected to catch this charm in a melodic organization, a number that could resound with the hearts of the people who heard it.

2. The Melodic Sythesis

"The Beluga's Ditty" started as a straightforward, tormenting tune, similar as the shocking calls of the actual belugas. It was created for a performance piano, the virtue of its sound mirroring the perfect idea of the Icy. The underlying tune was slow and pondering, reflecting the relaxed speed of life in the subarctic waters. It was made in a minor key to convey the feeling of yearning and despairing frequently connected with the tremendous, frigid scenes.

The creation was then extended to incorporate a little outfit, integrating strings, woodwinds, and, most strikingly, a performance woodwind. The flute was picked for its capacity to copy the assorted vocalizations of the beluga, delivering sounds that went from delicate, hoarse notes to additional extravagant quavers. The strings and woodwinds added profundity and warmth to the piece, portraying the Icy seascape.

3. **The Verses**

To bring the pith of the beluga whale and its reality to life, "The Beluga's Ditty" highlights reminiscent verses that portray the narrative of these enthralling marine warm blooded animals. The verses convey the regular routine of the beluga, its relationship with its unit, and the exceptional vocalizations that characterize its presence.

The verses proceed to praise the beluga's vocal abilities, its communications with other ocean animals, and its profound association with the always changing seascape of the North. It is a graceful tribute to the beluga, repeating its melodic presence on the planet's seas.

III. The Narrating through Music

1. **The Beluga's Excursion**

"The Beluga's Number" is a melodic structure that recounts a story. It starts by catching the beluga's excursion through the Icy waters, the piano directing the audience through the frosty profundities. The strings and woodwinds participate, reflecting the beluga's elegant developments as it skims through the perfectly clear sea.

As the music unfurls, it moves the audience to the core of the beluga case. The gathering's aggregate voices mirror the agreeable and social nature of these animals. The songs rise and fall like the delicate influxes of the Icy Sea, making a feeling of solidarity and reason inside the unit.

2. **The Cold Scene**

The song likewise portrays the Icy seascape. The verses and music portray the stunning excellence of the ice-shrouded waters, the moving Aurora Borealis, and the flawless appeal of the normal world. The flute, with its great many apparent varieties, catches the pith of the Cold climate, from the delicate, forlorn calls of the belugas to the fun loving, twittering hints of their associations.

As the organization arrives at its apex, it embodies the always changing light of the Icy, from the delicate shades of day break to the energetic splendor of the 12 PM sun. The audience is shipped to a domain where time appears to stop, and the significant excellence of the normal world is enlightened.

3. **The Beluga's Versatility**

"The Beluga's Number" isn't just about excellence and peacefulness; it likewise features the difficulties looked by the beluga whale in an impacting world. The music turns out to be more solemn as it mirrors the affliction that belugas stand up to, for example, environment corruption, expanded delivery traffic, and the effects of environmental change.

Be that as it may, even despite these difficulties, the song accentuates the beluga's versatility. The song gets back to its underlying, consoling notes, reminding the audience that the soul of the beluga perseveres. The piece leaves the crowd with a feeling of trust, that assuming we regard and safeguard the normal world, the sorcery of the Icy and the beluga's persevering through soul will continue.

IV. The Profound Effect

1. **A Calming and Intelligent Experience**

   "The Beluga's Melody" is most importantly a song, expected to be relieving and intelligent. Its delicate, melodic movement and the utilization of agreeable instruments make a feeling of serenity, welcoming the audience to relinquish pressure and track down comfort in the music.

   The piece's sluggish beat and delicate elements reflect the slow speed of life in the Icy, where everything moves at its own, deliberate cadence. Paying attention to this number is much the same as being drenched in the quieting embrace of the Cold ocean, no problem at all in the core of the beluga unit.

2. **An Association with Nature**

   One of the essential targets of "The Beluga's Melody" is to encourage a more profound association with nature. By wrapping the audience in the Icy's captivating soundscape, the number energizes consideration and reflection on the magnificence of our planet's northernmost scopes. It fills in as an update that we are all essential for the very worldwide environment and that our activities significantly affect the regular world.

   The music rouses sympathy for the beluga and its battle for endurance, which, thus, can propel people to help preservation endeavors and settle on decisions that benefit the climate.

3. **An Outflow of Workmanship and Inventiveness**

"The Beluga's Ditty" is a demonstration of the force of workmanship and imagination in conveying complex feelings and thoughts. Through the structure of this melody, the excellence and delicacy of the Cold biological system show some signs of life such that words alone would never catch.

This creative articulation makes a way for a reality where feeling, excellence, and understanding converge into one. It is an update that workmanship, in the entirety of its structures, can act as a scaffold between the human experience and the normal world.

4.1 Introduction to the Beluga Whale

The Beluga whale (Delphinapterus leucas), frequently alluded to as the "canary of the ocean" because of its charming vocalizations, is perhaps of the most particular and adored marine warm blooded animal on the planet. These effortless, white whales have caught the creative mind of individuals for quite a long time, and their extraordinary qualities and ways of behaving make them a subject of interest for scientists and nature lovers the same. In this 1600-word presentation, we will dig into the universe of the Beluga whale, investigating its actual characteristics, territory, ways of behaving, and preservation status.

1. ### Actual Attributes

Beluga whales are immediately unmistakable because of their striking actual elements, which put them aside from different cetaceans. Understanding these traits is fundamental to valuing the uniqueness of this species.

1. ### Hue
   One of the most striking highlights of Beluga whales is their unblemished white or light dark hue. This obvious white appearance, particularly in mature grown-ups, remains as a distinct difference to the dull, dark blue of the sea and is a central quality of the species. This shading is a transformation to their cold living space, giving cover in the transcendently white climate of the Icy and subarctic waters.

2. ### Absence of Dorsal Blade
   Belugas don't have a dorsal blade, which is a typical quality of numerous other whale species. All things considered, they have a little, bump like edge on their backs. This transformation permits them to move effectively underneath the endlessly ice floes, diminishing the gamble of getting caught under it.

3. **Adjusted Brow or Melon**

The particular, adjusted brow of the Beluga whale, frequently alluded to as the "melon," houses the whale's echolocation organs. These organs empower the Beluga to discharge and get sound waves, which are vital for route and correspondence submerged. The melon is adaptable and can change shape, permitting the whale to concentrate and direct its vocalizations with accuracy.

4. **Size and Weight**

Beluga whales are viewed as medium-sized toothed whales, with guys ordinarily being bigger than females. Guys can develop to associate with 13 to 20 feet long and regularly weigh somewhere in the range of 1,100 and 3,500 pounds, while females are somewhat more modest. Infant Beluga calves are brought into the world at a typical length of 4.5 to 5.5 feet and can weigh around 150 pounds.

II. Environment and Reach

Beluga whales are dominatingly tracked down in the Cold and subarctic districts of the Northern Half of the globe, enveloping a huge and different scope of natural surroundings.

1. **Cold Reach**

Most of Beluga whales occupy the Cold locale, with populaces tracked down in the Icy Sea, the Bering Ocean, the Chukchi Ocean, and the Beaufort Ocean. Their broad reach stretches out to the waterfront waters of Gold country, Canada, Greenland, Norway, and Russia, making them perhaps of the most generally circulated cetacean specie in the Cold.

2. **Subarctic Reach**

Notwithstanding the Cold, Beluga whales can likewise be tracked down in subarctic locales. They are known to occupy the St. Lawrence Stream estuary in Canada, which gives an extraordinary open door to specialists to study and notice them in a more calm climate. The Beluga's presence in this locale is a demonstration of their versatility to shifting water temperatures.

3. **Occasional Movement**

Belugas are known for their occasional movements inside their reach. They follow the development of ice to get to their favored environments, which might change with the seasons. Throughout the mid year months, they frequently move further north, following the subsiding ice to arrive at their taking care of grounds.

III. Ways of behaving and Variations

Beluga whales display a large number of ways of behaving and variations that make them appropriate to their Cold and subarctic living spaces.

1. **Social Design**

   Belugas are profoundly friendly creatures, frequently framing very close gatherings known as cases. These units can differ in size from only a couple of people to more than 1,000 individuals, contingent upon the area and the season. These units give security, hunting open doors, and social communication for the whales.

2. **Vocalizations**

   One of the most amazing elements of Beluga whales is their vocalizations. They are known for their different and complex collection of sounds, which incorporate whistles, snaps, twitters, and even tunes. These vocalizations fill different needs, including correspondence inside the unit, planning exercises, mingling, and possibly distinguishing people.

   Beluga melodies are especially fascinating, frequently going on for minutes and highlighting complicated examples of sound. These melodies are accepted to assume a pivotal part in the whales' social communications and might be utilized for mating and laying an out area.

3. **Taking care of**
   Beluga whales are deft feeders, meaning they devour a wide assortment of prey contingent upon their area and food accessibility. Their essential eating regimen comprises of fish, with species like Cold cod, capelin, and herring being normal prey things. They likewise feed on squid and different benthic spineless creatures. Their capacity to adjust to changing food sources is fundamental for their endurance in the difficult Icy climate, where prey accessibility can vary occasionally and yearly.

4. **Transformations for Cold Life**

Beluga whales have a few physical and conduct variations that make them appropriate for life in the Cold. Their thick layer of fat, for instance, gives protection and lightness in the virus waters while likewise filling in as an energy store for long movements and times of fasting.

Their absence of a dorsal blade and their adaptable melon make them light-footed swimmers, empowering them to explore through restricted spaces and under ice effortlessly. Furthermore, their capacity to express and involve echolocation is an imperative transformation for hunting and conveying in the frequently dinky Icy waters.

IV. Preservation Status

The preservation status of Beluga whales differs relying upon the populace and area, however generally speaking, they face a scope of dangers that require cautious observing and protection endeavors.

1. **Dangers**
   Beluga whales are presented to various dangers, including:
   Environmental Change: As environmental change speeds up, the Cold is encountering climbing temperatures, which brings about the liquefying of ocean ice. This influences the Beluga's natural surroundings and can prompt changes in their circulation and taking care of examples.
   Environment Corruption: Human exercises, like transportation

traffic and modern turn of events, can prompt territory debasement and unsettling influence of Beluga populaces. Expanded commotion contamination from vessels can slow down their correspondence and echolocation.

Hunting: Beluga hunting has happened generally in certain districts for their meat, skin, and lard. While hunting is directed and overseen in numerous areas, it stays a worry for explicit populaces.

Contamination: Contamination from different sources, remembering modern overflow and toxins for prey species, can influence the strength of Beluga populaces. This incorporates openness to weighty metals and synthetic compounds that can gather in their tissues.

2. **Protection Endeavors**

Preservation endeavors are progressing to safeguard Beluga whales and their Icy and subarctic natural surroundings. These endeavors include:

Examination and Checking: Researchers and scientists concentrate on Beluga populaces to acquire a superior comprehension of their dispersion, ways of behaving, and wellbeing. This data is crucial for successful protection the board.

Safeguarded Regions: The foundation of marine safeguarded regions and untamed life saves helps defend significant Beluga environments from human effects.

Guideline and Regulation: Public and global guidelines, for example, the Marine Warm blooded animal Assurance Act in the US and arrangements between Icy countries, assist with shielding Beluga populaces from overhunting and different dangers.

Environmental Change Alleviation: Endeavors to decrease ozone depleting substance emanations and relieve environmental change are pivotal for saving Beluga whale natural surroundings in the Cold.

Public Mindfulness: Raising public mindfulness about the significance of Beluga whale preservation and the need to safeguard their living spaces is fundamental for collecting backing and encouraging capable way of behaving.

4.2 The Melodic Calls of Belugas

The Beluga whale, otherwise called the "canary of the ocean" because of its captivating vocalizations, is perhaps of the most unmistakable marine warm blooded animal on the planet. Belugas are known for their momentous capacity to deliver a wide cluster of sounds, from musical tunes to complicated snaps and whistles. These vocalizations are not just a method for correspondence inside their gatherings yet additionally a wellspring of interest for specialists and a demonstration of the perplexing and dynamic universe of these charming marine vertebrates. In this 1500-word investigation, we will dig into the melodic calls of Belugas, digging into their importance, variety, and the bits of knowledge they give into the existences of these baffling animals.

1. ### The Murmurs of the Cold: Figuring out Beluga Vocalizations
1. **The Force of Sound**

   Sound is the essential medium through which Beluga whales communicate with their current circumstance and one another. Inside the sea's profundities, where perceivability is in many cases restricted, sound takes on a significant significance. The vocalizations of Belugas are fundamental for correspondence, route, hunting, and social holding.

2. **Sorts of Vocalizations**

   Beluga vocalizations envelop a wide range of sounds, each filling explicit needs. These vocalizations can be comprehensively ordered into the accompanying sorts:

   Whistles: Whistles are sharp sounds with unmistakable examples. Belugas use whistles for social correspondence, for example, recognizing themselves to different individuals from their case. Every Beluga has its one of a kind whistle, much the same as a name, and this singular distinguishing proof assumes an essential part in their social design.

Clicks: Snaps are fast, short explosions of sound delivered by Belugas. These sounds serve principally for echolocation, assisting the whales with exploring, track down food, and investigate their current circumstance. Clicks are frequently compared to the sonar frameworks utilized in submarines, permitting Belugas to "see" through sound.

Tunes: Beluga melodies are maybe the most hypnotizing of their vocalizations. These tunes comprise of a progression of sounds, frequently including perplexing examples and rhythms. While the specific reason for tunes is as yet a subject of exploration, they are accepted to play a part in mating, laying an out area, or keeping up with social bonds inside the unit.

3. **Vocal Learning and Intricacy**

One of the astounding parts of Beluga vocalizations is their intricacy and limit with regards to vocal learning. They are fit for imitating and learning new sounds, including those from different species and, surprisingly, human-made clamors. This versatility exhibits their insight and the extravagance of their acoustic collection.

II. Beluga Vocalizations and Social Bonds

1. **Unit Correspondence**
Beluga whales are profoundly friendly creatures, and their vocalizations assume an essential part in keeping up with the cohesiveness of their cases. Cases are normally comprised of firmly related people, and these family securities are supported through vocal correspondence. The acknowledgment of explicit whistles empowers Belugas to remain associated with their relatives and direction exercises inside the case.

2. **Sharing Feelings**
Belugas are known to communicate their feelings through

vocalizations. These vocalizations are a method for passing on data as well as an approach to communicating euphoria, fervor, or pain. Their tunes and whistles can turn out to be especially pleasant during snapshots of festivity or play, and alternately, they might turn out to be more repressed during seasons of grieving or stress.

3. **Mating Calls**

Beluga tunes are accepted to assume a huge part in romance and mating. During the rearing season, guys might sing to draw in females and lay out their domain. The intricacy and variety in their melodies might act as a type of sexual choice, with females leaning toward guys who can deliver the most unpredictable and enthralling tunes.

III. The Secret of Beluga Tunes

1. **Tune Design**
   Beluga tunes are portrayed by their mind boggling and different design. These tunes comprise of a progression of sounds, including whistles, peeps, and different vocalizations, organized in complex examples. The request and timing of these sounds can change, and the actual melodies can traverse a few minutes.

2. **Geographic Fluctuation**
   One of the most captivating parts of Beluga tunes is their geographic changeability. Various populaces of Belugas in different locales display unmistakable melody designs. This geographic changeability might be impacted by various variables, remembering the requirement for various correspondence systems for their particular surroundings.

3. **The Job of Melodies**

The exact reason for Beluga melodies stays a subject of progressing exploration and discussion. While melodies probably assume a part in mating, they may likewise serve different capabilities, for example, laying an out area, keeping up with social bonds, or communicating feelings. The intricacy and uniqueness of Beluga melodies recommend that they are a method for correspondence and articulation with various layers of importance.

IV. Exploration and Protection Suggestions

1. Concentrating on Beluga Vocalizations

The investigation of Beluga vocalizations has given significant bits of knowledge into their way of behaving, social design, and nature. Analysts use hydrophones and submerged recording gear to catch and examine the sounds created by these whales. The information gathered through acoustic exploration has added to a more profound comprehension of their lives and has opened new roads for protection endeavors.

2. Preservation Concerns

Beluga populaces face different dangers, including environmental change, living space corruption, modern turn of events, delivering traffic, and hunting in certain areas. Understanding their vocalizations and how they utilize sound in their current circumstance is fundamental for creating techniques to safeguard them.

3. Acoustic Biology

The field of acoustic biology centers around the job of sound in regular biological systems and what human exercises mean for the acoustic climate. The investigation of Beluga vocalizations is a necessary piece of acoustic environment, revealing insight into the results of clamor contamination in the seas. Human-produced commotion from transportation, modern action, and sporting drifting can disturb Beluga correspondence, route, and hunting, featuring the requirement for capable practices in marine conditions.

4. Public Mindfulness and Backing

The spellbinding idea of Beluga vocalizations fills in as a useful asset for raising public mindfulness about the protection of these heavenly animals and the significance of saving their natural surroundings. By sharing the excellence and intricacy of Beluga tunes, specialists and moderates can draw in general society in endeavors to safeguard these wonderful marine warm blooded animals and the seas they call home.

4.3 The Life of Beluga Whales in the Arctic

The Cold, a tremendous and freezing territory of ice and water, is home to a portion of the world's most noteworthy and perplexing animals, including the Beluga whale (Delphinapterus leucas). These immaculate, white marine warm blooded animals, frequently alluded to as the "canaries of the ocean" for their musical vocalizations, are exceptionally adjusted to life in this outrageous climate. In this 600-word investigation, we will dive into the existence of Beluga whales in the Icy, revealing insight into their living space, ways of behaving, and astounding transformations that empower them to flourish on the planet's northernmost oceans.

1. Cold Natural surroundings: A Difficult Home

The Cold is a locale of limits, described by lengthy, brutal winters with bone chilling temperatures and broad ocean ice. In this climate, Beluga whales explore a bunch of difficulties that request unique transformations.

1. **Ice-Covered Waters**
   One of the characterizing elements of the Cold is its ice-shrouded waters, which are canvassed in ocean ice for a huge piece of the year. Belugas should have the option to move through this ice to get to their hunting grounds and explore their extensive territory.
2. **Changing Seasons**
   The Cold encounters sensational occasional movements, from the polar evening of winter to the 12 PM sun of summer. Belugas

are adjusted to these changes, with relocations because of moving ice and temperature varieties.

3. **Ruthless Difficulties**

Belugas are sharp feeders, going after different types of fish, squid, and spineless creatures. Their essential prey incorporates Icy cod, capelin, herring, and other marine animals. Their eating routine differs in view of area and occasional accessibility, making them adaptable trackers.

II. Social Design: The Significance of Units

Belugas are profoundly friendly animals and structure very close gatherings known as units. These cases act as fundamental social units and give various advantages to the whales in the difficult Icy climate.

1. **Family Bonds**
   Beluga units frequently comprise of firmly related people, including moms, calves, and other relatives. These family bonds are fundamental for the insurance and endurance of the youthful and act as a social emotionally supportive network for all individuals.

2. **Correspondence and Collaboration**
   Inside these units, Belugas participate in mind boggling vocalizations, including whistles, snaps, and melodies, which are crucial for correspondence, coordination of exercises, and social holding. The capacity to distinguish and answer the particular whistles of unit individuals is critical for keeping up with bunch attachment.

3. **Predation Protection**

The aggregate strength of a unit is a powerful safeguard against likely hunters, for example, polar bears and executioner whales. The unit can cooperate to deflect or safeguard against dangers, giving an additional layer of safety in the difficult Cold climate.

III. Vocalizations: The Songs of the Ocean

Beluga whales are known for their momentous vocalizations, which assume a focal part in their lives and connections inside the case. Their vocal collection incorporates whistles, snaps, tweets, and tunes, and each kind of sound fills an exceptional need.

1. **Whistles**

   Whistles are shrill sounds with particular examples. Belugas use whistles for social correspondence, for example, distinguishing themselves to different individuals from their unit. Every Beluga has its interesting whistle, working like a name that encourages individual acknowledgment.

2. **Clicks**

   Clicks are quick, short eruptions of sound delivered by Belugas. These sounds are utilized for echolocation, assisting the whales with exploring, track down food, and investigate their current circumstance. Clicks give them a hear-able "map" of their environmental factors, similar to a type of submerged sonar.

3. **Tunes**

Beluga tunes are among the most enthralling vocalizations delivered by these marine vertebrates. These tunes comprise of a progression of sounds, frequently including complicated examples and rhythms. While the exact reason for tunes stays a subject of exploration and discussion, they are accepted to play a part in mating, an area foundation, or social holding inside the case.

IV. Step by step processes for surviving: Transformations to the Icy

Belugas have developed a bunch of variations to get by and flourish in the difficult Icy climate, both in the water and on the ice.

1. **Lard Layer**

   One of the most pivotal variations is their thick layer of fat, which gives protection and lightness in the virus waters while filling in as an energy store. This lard layer assists with saving body heat, guaranteeing the whales stay warm and protected in the bone chilling Cold oceans.

2. **Absence of Dorsal Balance**

   Not at all like numerous other whale species, Belugas come up short on dorsal blade. This transformation empowers them to explore through restricted spaces and under ice all the more effectively, diminishing the gamble of getting caught underneath ice floes.

3. **Melon**

   The "melon," an unmistakable, adjusted brow lodging echolocation organs, is a flexible transformation that permits Belugas to emanate and get sound waves. The adaptable melon can change shape, empowering the whales to concentrate and direct their vocalizations with accuracy.

4. **Vocal Learning**

Belugas show striking vocal abilities to learn, fit for mirroring and learning new sounds, including those from different species and, surprisingly, human-made commotions. This flexibility shows their insight and the lavishness of their acoustic collection.

V. Protection Difficulties

While Belugas have adjusted to the Icy's difficulties, they face different dangers to their populaces, basically coming from human exercises and environmental change.

1. **Environmental Change**

   Fast warming in the Icy district is causing the softening of ocean ice, which can modify Belugas' living space and taking care of examples. These progressions influence their capacity to get to food and explore their current circumstance.

2. **Territory Corruption**

   Delivering traffic, modern turn of events, and human unsettling influence can prompt territory debasement and upset Beluga populaces. Expanded commotion contamination from vessels can disrupt their correspondence, route, and hunting.

3. Protection Endeavors

Endeavors are in progress to safeguard Beluga whales and their Icy living spaces. Specialists and protectionists are concentrating on these marine well evolved creatures to acquire a superior comprehension of their dissemination, ways of behaving, and wellbeing. Guidelines and arrangements are set up to oversee hunting and alleviate human effects on these animals.

4.4 A Beluga-inspired Lullaby

In the peaceful domain of the Icy oceans, where the unending territory of ice meets the quiet waters, the Beluga whale, frequently alluded to as the "canary of the ocean," graces us with its captivating presence. These flawless, white marine vertebrates, with their special transformations and sweet vocalizations, have propelled stunningness and appreciation for a really long time. In the soul of this exceptional animal, let us leave on a melodic excursion into the formation of a Beluga-roused children's song, a melody to the ocean's canaries that brings out the wizardry and peacefulness of the Cold waters.

1. **The Canaries of the Ocean**
   Beluga whales, with their particular white tinge and absence of dorsal balances, are really the canaries of the ocean. Similarly as the canary's tune has for quite some time been an image of excellence and concordance, the Beluga's vocalizations have caught the hearts of the people who have had the honor of hearing their melodic calls. These captivating vocalizations act as a wellspring of motivation for the production of a bedtime song, welcoming us to drench ourselves in the quietness of the Cold world.

2. **The Melodic Motivation**
   The formation of a Beluga-motivated cradlesong starts with the

melodic motivation drawn from the whales' own vocalizations. Beluga melodies, with their unpredictable examples and delicate rhythms, give the ideal establishment to a cradlesong that encapsulates the effortlessness and serenity of these brilliant animals.

The children's song's tune is suggestive of the frightful whistles and relieving snaps of Beluga vocalizations. A song reflects the delicate influencing of the whales as they skim through the Icy waters, offering a feeling of harmony and comfort. The selection of instruments, including piano and strings, further adds to the children's song's ethereal and amicable quality.

3. **The Verses: A Lovely Tribute**

   To finish the Beluga-enlivened cradlesong, reminiscent verses are made to convey the pith of the Beluga whale's life in the Icy oceans. These verses act as a lovely tribute to the glorious animals, praising their reality and their persevering through soul.

   The verses portray the tale of Beluga whales in their immaculate Cold living space, where ice and ocean meet fitting together beautifully. They depict the whales' effortless developments through the perfectly clear waters and their social collaborations inside the affectionate cases. The verses catch the melodic substance of Beluga vocalizations, permitting audience members to feel like they are drenched in the delicate song of the ocean's canaries.

   The verses proceed to commend the getting through soul of Beluga whales, helping us to remember the significance of saving the Cold climate and the astounding animals that call it home.

4. **The Close to home Association**

   A Beluga-roused cradlesong goes past the production of delightful music; it manufactures a profound close to home association between the audience and the normal world. The calming song, joined with suggestive verses, conjures a feeling of harmony, marvel, and appreciation for the Icy's magnificence and the existence it supports.

   Paying attention to the bedtime song ships the crowd to the

Cold's frozen hug, where time stops, and the world is enclosed by calm marvel. It is an encouragement to encounter the charm of the Beluga's reality, where the excellence of the ocean's canaries blends with the peacefulness of the Cold.

5. A Message of Preservation

A Beluga-motivated bedtime song fills in as an impactful sign of the difficulties that Beluga whales face in the impacting scene. Their perfect Cold living space is under danger from environmental change, territory corruption, transporting traffic, and modern turn of events. The children's song, with its suggestive tunes and sincere verses, conveys a message of protection and regard for the normal world.

It urges audience members to become advocates for the insurance of these amazing animals and their delicate biological systems. Through the cradlesong's delicate song, it is trusted that individuals will be roused to pursue decisions that benefit the climate and add to the safeguarding of the Cold's flawless magnificence.

5

Chapter 5

The Polar Bear's Hush

The Cold, an immense, confounding scope of ice and snow, is home to a portion of the World's most notorious and stunning animals. Among them, the polar bear (Ursus maritimus) remains as the undisputed lord of the frozen north. With its huge height, protecting fur, and marvelous hunting abilities, this dominant hunter rules over the cold wild.

However, the polar bear's domain is one of extraordinary magnificence and delicacy, and it faces exceptional difficulties in an impacting world. This 3000-word investigation, "The Polar Bear's Quiet," welcomes you to dive profound into the life, natural surroundings, conduct, and preservation status of these great animals. It is an excursion into the Icy domain, where the quieted universe of the polar bear unfurls before your eyes.

1. **The Icy Shelter**
1. **The Icy Biological system**
   The Icy, described by its cruel environment, cold waters, and flawless scenes, is a domain of exceptional magnificence. Here,

the Icy biological system flourishes, adjusted to outrageous circumstances, where ice rules for a critical piece of the year. This climate, while apparently fruitless, abounds with life, from tiny creatures in the ocean ice to the powerful hunters that tail the freezing waters and cold scenes.

2. The Notorious Polar Bear

The Icy's most famous and significant occupant is the polar bear, an image of solidarity and flexibility in a universe of ice and snow. These brilliant animals are worked to endure the unforgiving Icy environment and are flawlessly adjusted to their current circumstance.

II. Actual Qualities

1. Transformations to the Virus

Polar bears have a variety of actual highlights that make them especially fit to the Icy's super virus. Their most prominent trademark is their thick fur, comprising of both external gatekeeper hairs and a thick undercoat, which keeps them warm in temperatures as low as - 40°F (- 40°C). Their fur seems white, an ideal disguise against the encompassing ice and snow.

2. Wonderful Swimmers

Polar bears are likewise uncommon swimmers, with webbed feet and solid appendages adjusted for exploring the freezing waters. They are known to cover huge distances by swimming and can remain lowered for expanded periods while hunting seals, their essential prey.

3. Size and Height

Polar bears are among the biggest carnivores on The planet, with guys arriving at loads of as much as 1,500 pounds (680 kilograms) and remaining more than 10 feet (3 meters) tall when on their rear legs. Their size is a demonstration of their situation as dominant hunters in the Cold.

III. Natural surroundings and Reach

1. The Frozen Oceans

The essential territory of polar bears is the ocean ice of the Icy Sea, where they chase seals and marine vertebrates. They are known to run across the ocean ice looking for food, following the developments of their prey and the occasional changes in ice cover.

2. Occasional Relocation

Polar bears embrace occasional movements, following the development and retreat of the ocean ice. During the colder months, they move further north to get to their favored hunting grounds, while in the hotter months, they might withdraw to land or remaining ice floes.

IV. Conduct and Science

1. Seal Predation

Polar bears are impressive trackers, with seals framing the main part of their eating regimen. They fundamentally target seals like ringed seals and hairy seals, going after them as they surface for air through breathing openings or ice breaks. The bears utilize their sharp feeling of smell and persistence to find and follow their prey.

2. Propagation

Polar bears are lone creatures, except for moms with offspring. Mating happens from April to June, and pregnant females enter a time of postponed implantation. They conceive an offspring in the colder time of year, with whelps normally numbering one to three. Mother polar bears are devoted parental figures, sustaining and showing their fledglings abilities to survive.

3. Hibernation and Fasting

During the sans ice season, when prey is scant, polar bears might get through fasting for broadened periods. They depend on their fat stores to support them, losing huge load during these lean times.

V. Preservation Status

1. **Environmental Change**

   Polar bears are significantly affected by environmental change, as the warming of the Icy prompts the decrease of ocean ice. As their essential hunting grounds contract and become less open, polar bears face the test of tracking down adequate food to support them. It is extended that, without mediation, polar bears will confront populace decreases in the next few decades.

2. **Human Action**

   Human movement in the Cold likewise represents a danger to polar bears. Expanded delivery and modern advancement can upset their environment and carry them into contact with people, prompting possible struggles. Furthermore, polar bears can be pursued in certain locales, despite the fact that hunting is directed and overseen in numerous areas to safeguard their populaces.

3. **Protection Endeavors**

Endeavors are in progress to safeguard polar bears and their Cold territories. Specialists and traditionalists concentrate on these dominant hunters to acquire a superior comprehension of their circulation, ways of behaving, and wellbeing. Peaceful accords and guidelines are set up to oversee hunting and alleviate human effects on these notable animals.

5.1 Introduction to the Polar Bear

The polar bear (Ursus maritimus) is the undisputed ruler of the Icy, epitomizing strength, flexibility, and endurance in one of the cruelest and most unforgiving conditions on The planet. These great animals are known for their huge size, protecting fur, and unparalleled hunting ability in the frozen wild of the Icy. In this 1500-word presentation, we will dig into the enthralling universe of polar bears, investigating their actual qualities, environment, ways of behaving, and the preservation challenges they face in a quickly evolving environment.

1. Actual Qualities

Polar bears are eminently adjusted to their frosty space, with a scope of actual qualities that prepare them for life in the bone chilling Cold.

1. Fur and Tinge

One of the most famous elements of polar bears is their thick fur, which comprises of two unmistakable layers. The external layer comprises of long, sleek gatekeeper hairs that repulse water, while the thick undercoat gives protection against the super virus. Their fur seems white, which fills in as an ideal disguise against the encompassing ice and snow.

2. Size and Height

Polar bears are among the biggest carnivores on The planet, with guys arriving at great sizes. Grown-up guys can weigh between 900 to 1,600 pounds (410 to 725 kilograms) and stand north of 10 feet (3 meters) tall when on their rear legs. These monster aspects are a demonstration of their situation as dominant hunters in the Icy.

3. Strong Appendages

Polar bears serious areas of strength for have durable appendages that empower them to cross the frigid territory and swim significant distances looking for prey. Their front paws are huge, expansive, and to some degree webbed, giving magnificent oars to swimming. Their rear appendages are strong and are utilized for balance and for pushing their monstrous bodies through the water.

4. Specific Paws

The bottoms of a polar bear's feet are canvassed in little, raised papillae and thick fur, furnishing them with foothold on ice and diminishing intensity misfortune through their paws. This transformation is significant for both crossing the dangerous ice and swimming in freezing waters.

II. Environment and Reach

1. The Frozen Oceans

The essential environment of polar bears is the ocean ice of the Icy Sea. They are marine well evolved creatures that depend on the ice as a stage for hunting seals, their essential prey. The frozen ocean fills in as the bears' taking care of and favorable places, making it fundamental for their endurance.

2. Occasional Relocation

Polar bears embrace occasional relocations, following the development and retreat of ocean ice. During the colder months, they move further north to get to their favored hunting grounds, while in the hotter months, they might withdraw to land or remaining ice floes. This example of relocation is driven by the accessibility of prey and the moving ice.

III. Ways of behaving and Science

1. Seal Predation

Polar bears are impressive trackers, with seals shaping the heft of their eating routine. They principally target seals like ringed seals and hairy seals, going after them as they surface for air through breathing openings or ice breaks. Polar bears utilize their sharp feeling of smell and persistence to find and follow their prey, frequently ready to pounce close to seal breathing openings.

2. Proliferation

Polar bears are singular creatures, aside from moms with whelps. Mating happens from April to June, and pregnant females enter a time of deferred implantation. They conceive an offspring in the colder time of year, with fledglings commonly numbering one to three. Mother polar bears are committed parental figures, supporting and showing their fledglings basic instincts.

3. Hibernation and Fasting

During the sans ice season, when prey is scant, polar bears might get through fasting for expanded periods. They depend on their fat stores to support them, losing critical load during these lean times. This fasting and metabolic variation empower them to get by in the unforgiving Cold climate, where food can be scant for quite some time.

IV. Preservation Status

1. Environmental Change

Polar bears are significantly impacted by environmental change, which prompts the decrease of ocean ice and influences their capacity to get to their essential hunting grounds. The Icy is warming at a sped up rate, prompting the downfall of ocean ice and a more limited hunting season for polar bears. This is a significant danger to their endurance, as they depend on seals for food, particularly during the without ice months.

2. Human Action

Human action in the Cold likewise represents a danger to polar bears. Expanded delivery and modern improvement can disturb their territory and carry them into contact with people, prompting likely struggles. Moreover, polar bears can be pursued in certain districts, in spite of the fact that hunting is controlled and overseen in numerous areas to safeguard their populaces.

3. Preservation Endeavors

Endeavors are in progress to safeguard polar bears and their Cold territories. Scientists and preservationists concentrate on these dominant hunters to acquire a superior comprehension of their dissemination, ways of behaving, and wellbeing. Peaceful accords and guidelines are set up to oversee hunting and relieve human effects on these famous animals. The predicament of polar bears is a source of inspiration, encouraging us to safeguard their environments and guarantee the endurance of these Icy goliaths.

5.2 The Silent World of Polar Bears

In the tremendous, frozen scenes of the Icy, a quiet and glorious world exists, governed by perhaps of Earth's most notable hunter — the polar bear (Ursus maritimus). These singular monsters of the ice have adjusted to a climate of tenacious cold, where quiet frequently rules. In this 1200-word investigation, we adventure into the quiet universe of polar bears, uncovering their amazing variations, ways of behaving, and the difficulties they face in a consistently changing Icy climate.

1. **A Quiet Space**

The Cold is a domain of stunning excellence, where the quietness of unending frosty scenes is just hindered by a periodic whirlwind or the squeaking of ocean ice. In this world, polar bears explore a quieted presence as they chase, breed, and get by in a place where there is ice and snow.

1. **The Frozen Natural surroundings**
   The Icy's super chilly, cold waters, and unblemished scenes make it the best natural surroundings for polar bears. Their essential space is the ocean ice of the Icy Sea, which they use as a stage for hunting seals, their essential prey. This frozen breadth fills in as their taking care of and favorable places, where the quiet of the Cold is accentuated simply by the hints of ice and water.
2. **Singular Hunters**

Polar bears are singular animals, except for moms with offspring. They spend quite a bit of their lives alone, looking for go after the huge ice floes, a glaring difference to the social ways of behaving of other bear species. Their lone nature is an impression of the shortage of food in the Cold and the need to keep away from rivalry with other polar bears.

II. Quiet Ways of behaving

Polar bears participate in a scope of ways of behaving that mirror the quiet world they possess, each activity finely tuned to their current circumstance and hunting techniques.

1. **The Specialty of Persistence**

   Polar bears are bosses of persistence, particularly with regards to hunting seals. They frequently lie on pause close to seal breathing openings or ice breaks, in some cases for quite a long time, until a seal surfaces for air. This quiet watchfulness is fundamental for their hunting achievement, as it permits them to preserve energy and hit with accuracy whenever the open door emerges.

2. **Quiet Following**

   The bears' quiet following abilities are unrivaled. They get across the ice with a liquid effortlessness that misrepresents their monstrous size, depending on their brilliant disguise and calm developments to move toward their prey without discovery. This secrecy is pivotal for getting seals, their essential food source.

3. **Quiet Correspondence**

While polar bears are commonly singular, they truly do speak with each other utilizing different quiet signals. Actual signals, like non-verbal communication and stances, assume a huge part in polar bear connections. A straightforward signal, similar to a brought down head or a raised paw, can convey strength or accommodation, diminishing the requirement for vocalizations.

III. Transformations for Quietness

Polar bears have a scope of actual transformations that help them in getting by and flourishing in the quiet Cold world.

1. **Protecting Fur**

   The bears' thick fur fills numerous needs, including protection against the super virus. It comprises of two layers: a water-repellent external layer of gatekeeper hairs and a thick, protecting undercoat. This fur keeps the bears warm, assists them with drifting in water, and gives a viable cover against the encompassing ice and snow.

2. **Covert Paw Cushions**

   The bottoms of a polar bear's feet are shrouded in little, raised papillae and thick fur, which give footing on ice and lessen heat misfortune through their paws. This variation is pivotal for navigating the dangerous ice quietly and following seals successfully.

3. **Insignificant Vocalizations**

Polar bears are moderately quiet animals, producing insignificant vocalizations contrasted with other bear species. They use vocalizations principally during mating or in mother-fledgling collaborations. Their restricted vocal reach is appropriate to an existence where quietness and secrecy are principal.

IV. Protection Difficulties

The quiet universe of polar bears is under danger, fundamentally because of environmental change and human exercises.

1. **Dissolving Ocean Ice**

   Environmental change is causing the quick warming of the Icy, prompting the dissolving of ocean ice. Subsequently, polar bears are confronting huge difficulties in getting to their essential hunting grounds. This prompts broadened fasting periods and diminished admittance to seals, which can bring about weight reduction, diminished offspring endurance rates, and populace decline.

2. **Human Movement**

   Expanded delivery and modern advancement in the Icy can

disturb polar bears' environments and carry them into contact with people. This vicinity can prompt expected clashes and expanded weight on bear populaces.

3. **Preservation Endeavors**

Endeavors are in progress to safeguard polar bears and their Cold territories. Specialists and traditionalists are concentrating on these dominant hunters to acquire a superior comprehension of their conveyance, ways of behaving, and wellbeing. Peaceful accords and guidelines are set up to oversee hunting and moderate human effects on these notable animals.

5.3 The Role of Polar Bears in the Arctic Food Chain

The Icy is an immense and novel biological system, known for its super chilly, flawless scenes, and exceptional natural life. At the head of the Cold pecking order stands the polar bear, a great dominant hunter that has adjusted to this brutal climate north of millions of years. Polar bears are charming images of the Icy, however they likewise assume a significant part in the Cold pecking order and environment. we will dig profound into the universe of polar bears and look at their importance in keeping up with the equilibrium of the Cold food web.

The Icy Biological system

1.1 Outline of the Cold Biological system

The Cold biological system is a perplexing trap of life that envelops different natural surroundings, including ocean ice, waterfront regions, tundra, and marine conditions. It is portrayed by outrageous cool, extensive stretches of dimness, and a somewhat short developing season. This section gives an outline of the Icy biological system, featuring remarkable elements and the difficulties living life forms face in this climate.

1.2 Biodiversity in the Icy

In spite of its brutal circumstances, the Icy is home to an astonishing assortment of living things, from minuscule green growth to huge vertebrates like polar bears. We will investigate the biodiversity of the

Icy, zeroing in on the species that polar bears cooperate with and rely upon for their endurance.

Polar Bears - The Notable Cold Hunters

2.1 Life structures and Transformations of Polar Bears

Polar bears are interestingly adjusted to the Icy climate. Their actual elements, conduct, and concentrated transformations make them exceptionally productive trackers and swimmers in frosty waters. This segment will dive into the life structures and variations of polar bears.

2.2 Life Cycle and Conduct

The existence cycle and conduct of polar bears are entrancing points. From their proliferation and maternal consideration to their hunting techniques and collaborations with different bears, this part will give an exhaustive comprehension of how polar bears live and make due in the Cold.

Taking care of Environment of Polar Bears

3.1 The Eating routine of Polar Bears

Polar bears are fundamentally predatory hunters, and their eating regimen is to a great extent reliant upon the accessibility of prey species in the Cold. We will investigate the different food sources that polar bears eat, with a specific spotlight on their principal prey - seals.

3.2 Seal Hunting Strategies

Polar bears are prestigious for their capacity to chase seals, particularly ringed seals and unshaven seals. This segment will detail the hunting procedures utilized by polar bears, including their wonderful seal-hunting strategies on ocean ice.

Polar Bears and the Cold Pecking order

4.1 Cornerstone Hunters

Polar bears are viewed as cornerstone hunters in the Cold pecking order. Their job goes past hunting; they significantly affect the whole biological system. This part will look at the meaning of polar bears as cornerstone hunters and how their presence or nonappearance can impact the Cold food web.

4.2 Polar Bears and Seal Populaces

The connection between polar bears and seals is at the core of the Icy pecking order. Changes in polar bear populaces can have flowing impacts on seal populaces, prompting more extensive biological outcomes. We will investigate this complex association and its suggestions.

Environmental Change and Polar Bears

5.1 Environmental Change in the Icy

The Icy is encountering the impacts of environmental change at a sped up rate. This part will examine the ecological difficulties presented by environmental change in the Cold, including ocean ice misfortune, temperature increments, and the ramifications for the whole biological system.

5.2 Effect of Environmental Change on Polar Bears

Polar bears are especially helpless against the impacts of environmental change. Decreased ocean ice and changed seal natural surroundings are straightforwardly affecting polar bear populaces. We will dive into the particular manners by which environmental change is influencing polar bears and their job in the Cold pecking order.

Preservation Endeavors and The board

6.1 Preservation Status of Polar Bears

Polar bears are named helpless, and their future is a subject of worry for researchers and traditionalists. In this section, we will investigate the ongoing preservation status of polar bears, including the dangers they face and the lawful securities set up.

6.2 Protection Techniques

Endeavors to ration polar bears include different methodologies, from territory security to peaceful accords. This part will frame the key preservation procedures and drives pointed toward guaranteeing the endurance of polar bears and their basic job in the Icy biological system.

The Interconnected Cold Biological system

7.1 Communications with Other Cold Species

Polar bears communicate with a scope of other Cold species, and these cooperations have more extensive ramifications for the biological system. We will inspect how polar bears impact the ways of behaving of different creatures and how these associations shape the Icy food web.

7.2 Flowing Consequences for the Cold Pecking order

The presence or nonappearance of polar bears can set off flowing impacts all through the Cold pecking order. This section will talk about these gradually expanding influences, remembering changes for prey populaces, changes in hunter conduct, and modifications in the general equilibrium of the environment.

Future Difficulties and Vulnerabilities

8.1 The Questionable Fate of Polar Bears

The eventual fate of polar bears is dubious, as they face various difficulties, from environmental change to anthropogenic effects. We will investigate the vulnerabilities encompassing polar bear populaces and their spot in the Icy pecking order.

8.2 The More extensive Ramifications

The decay of polar bears could have expansive ramifications for the Icy environment and even effect worldwide environment frameworks. This segment will examine the more extensive ramifications of polar bear preservation and the job they play in keeping a decent Icy food web.

5.4 A Polar Bear-inspired Lullaby

In the peaceful, snow-shrouded scenes of the Icy, quite possibly of the most famous and dazzling animal rules: the polar bear. These glorious creatures, impeccably adjusted to the unforgiving states of their frigid world, have long caught the creative mind of individuals all around the globe. Their colossal strength, versatile soul, and exquisite presence have made them an image of the frozen wild, as well as a demonstration of the significance of preservation notwithstanding environmental change.

However, imagine a scenario where we were to dig into the polar bear's reality not through logical texts or narratives, but rather through the mitigating, charming tunes of a children's song. This 15,000-word investigation takes you on an inspiring excursion through the Cold, where the polar bear's life and its charming environmental elements become the background for a bedtime song that catches the actual quintessence of this phenomenal creature. As we leave on this melodious journey, we'll find the significant association between the Icy climate and the polar bear's presence, all enveloped by the delicate hug of a polar bear-enlivened bedtime song.

The Cold's Frozen Embroidery

The Cold, a place where there is unending ice and snow, is an extraordinary domain where the components plot to make a position of ethereal excellence and unforgiving cruelty. In this part, we set the stage by diving into the Cold's enamoring scene, portraying the stunning icy masses, the gleaming auroras, and the significant tranquility of its huge, white region.

The Polar Bear's Realm

This section brings us profound into the core of the Icy to investigate the polar bear's reality. We find out about the bear's variations for endurance, from its protecting fur to its strong paws, and how these transformations have developed over the long haul. We likewise reveal the polar bear's job as the dominant hunter of the Icy and its fundamental association with the marine biological system.

Cold Evenings

As we plunge into the universe of the polar bear, we find that life in the Icy isn't just about the constant cold and snow; it's likewise a position of significant quietness and peacefulness. The Cold evenings, with their ritzy skies and the weak, otherworldly gleam of Aurora Borealis, make an air that rouses our children's song.

A Mother's Adoration

In this part, we investigate the existence of a polar bear mother as she supports her whelps. We dig into the cozy minutes among mother and kid, uncovering the delicate and defensive side of these strong animals. The cradlesong starts to come to fruition as we mull over the profundity of a mother's affection.

The Dance of the Ice

The Cold's frozen scenes are not static however steadily evolving. Ice floes float, glacial masses calve, and the ocean ice shifts with the tides. This part investigates the powerful idea of the Cold's frosty stage, where the polar bear's life unfurls. The cradlesong mirrors this consistently moving dance in its songs.

The Tune of Endurance

The polar bear's life is one of steady transformation and endurance. In this part, we dig into the bear's hunting strategies, its single nature, and its tireless mission for food. The children's song turns into an impression of the bear's flexibility and assurance.

Confronting the Pit

Environmental change represents an existential danger to the polar bear, as the dissolving ice compromises its actual presence. This part investigates the significant difficulties that the polar bear faces in the changing Icy climate. The cradlesong takes on a melancholy note, mirroring the criticalness of protection endeavors.

The Confident Note

In the midst of the difficulties, there is trust. In this part, we investigate the preservation endeavors and drives pointed toward protecting the polar bear and its environment. We track down motivation in the devotion of researchers, activists, and networks attempting to safeguard these magnificent animals. The cradlesong's song starts to move, conveying a message of trust.

A Bedtime song for the Cold

As we approach the finish of our excursion, the cradlesong motivated by the polar bear and the Cold comes to fruition. We unite every one of the components we've investigated, from the frosty scenes to the bear's perseverance, from the maternal love to the moving dance of the ice. The cradlesong winds around a story of the Icy, the polar bear, and the critical need to safeguard this delicate environment.

The Tune of Protection

In the last part, we ponder the meaning of the cradlesong, as a relieving tune as well as a source of inspiration. We underscore the significance of rationing the Icy and its exceptional occupants, and how the cradlesong can act as an image of this responsibility. We end our excursion with a call for change, motivating expectation and activity despite an evolving environment.

Chapter 6

The Arctic Fox's Serenade

The Icy Fox, experimentally known as Vulpes lagopus, is an entrancing animal of the far northern compasses of our planet. Dwelling in the unforgiving Cold tundra and the high sloping locales of the Northern Half of the globe, this confounding canine has spellbound the creative mind of researchers and nature fans for ages. Known for its exceptional versatility to outrageous environments and its striking white fur, the Icy Fox is a meaningful figure of the Cold wild, epitomizing the actual substance of endurance in perhaps of the most brutal climate on The planet.

In this paper, we leave on an excursion to grasp the life and extraordinary qualities of the Icy Fox, with a specific spotlight on its vocalizations - frequently alluded to as the "Icy Fox's Song." We will investigate the nature and conduct of this species, revealing insight into the methodologies it utilizes to flourish in such a difficult climate. We will likewise dive into the vocalizations of the Cold Fox, their capabilities, and the job they play in the many-sided public activities of these tricky animals. Moreover, we will examine the difficulties and dangers that the Cold

Fox faces in an impacting world, underlining the significance of preservation endeavors to safeguard this famous species.

Cold Fox Biology and Conduct

1.1 Environment and Circulation:

The Cold Fox has a circumpolar conveyance, occupying probably the most remote and unwelcoming districts of the Northern Half of the globe. This segment will give an outline of the different natural surroundings it involves and how its way of behaving adjusts to these difficult conditions.

1.2 Actual Transformations:

The Icy Fox has a momentous set-up of actual transformations, from its thick fur garment to its little size and unmistakable paws. This segment investigates how these transformations empower it to get by in the unforgiving Icy circumstances.

1.3 Eating regimen and Hunting Methodologies:

Understanding the eating regimen and hunting techniques for the Icy Fox is vital to valuing its environmental job. This segment dives into the prey species it targets, hunting procedures, and occasional varieties in its eating routine.

1.4 Propagation and Life Cycle:

The Cold Fox's life cycle is intently attached to the outrageous irregularity of its current circumstance. This part investigates its reproducing propensities, the difficulties of raising youthful in the Icy, and the procedures utilized to guarantee the endurance of its posterity.

The Cold Fox's Melody - Vocalizations and Correspondence

2.1 Vocal Collection:

The Icy Fox is known for its assorted vocalizations, frequently alluded to as a "serenade." In this part, we dig into the various kinds of vocalizations, including barks, howls, and shouts, and their importance in the fox's life.

2.2 Social Construction and Correspondence:

The Icy Fox is certainly not a lone creature and depends on friendly cooperations for different parts of its life. We analyze the social construction and specialized strategies utilized by these creatures to facilitate and communicate inside their gatherings.

2.3 Meaning of Vocalizations:

The "Icy Fox's Song" is something beyond clamor; it serves basic capabilities inside the Icy Fox's social design, including mating ceremonies, region safeguard, and correspondence among guardians and posterity. This part investigates the different settings where vocalizations are utilized.

Preservation Difficulties and Endeavors

3.1 Dangers to Cold Fox Populaces:

The Cold Fox faces a bunch of difficulties in the cutting edge world, from environmental change and territory misfortune to predation and illnesses. This part examines the significant dangers to Icy Fox populaces and their effect.

3.2 Protection Endeavors:

Endeavors to monitor the Icy Fox are imperative to guaranteeing the species' endurance in a steadily impacting world. We will look at progressing preservation drives, including research, hostage rearing projects, and environment assurance, and their effect on these amazing animals.

3.3 The Moral Quandary:

Preservation choices frequently include moral contemplations, like the expected effect on different species and biological systems. This part tends to the moral predicaments related with safeguarding the Cold Fox and its living space.

6.1 Introduction to the Arctic Fox

The Cold fox (Vulpes lagopus), frequently alluded to as the polar fox or snow fox, is a striking and versatile animal types that has adjusted to perhaps of the most extreme climate on The planet - the Icy tundra. This little flesh eater, known for its immaculate white fur and shaggy tail, is a famous inhabitant of the polar districts and has enthralled the creative mind of researchers, preservationists, and nature devotees the same. In this paper, we will dive into the universe of the Cold fox, investigating its actual qualities, environment, conduct, transformations, and preservation status. Through a far reaching comprehension of this striking species, we can acquire experiences into the difficulties and potential open doors it faces in an impacting world.

Actual Qualities

The Cold fox is a moderately little well evolved creature, regularly gauging between 3 to 9 pounds (1.4 to 4.1 kilograms) and estimating around 18 to 27 inches (46 to 68 centimeters) in body length, with a tail adding an extra 11 to 21 inches (28 to 53 centimeters) to its general length. These aspects are appropriate for the fox's Icy territory, permitting it to save heat while staying deft in the snow.

One of the most striking highlights of the Cold fox is its fur, which changes tone with the seasons. Throughout the cold weather months, its fur is thick and snow-white, giving extraordinary disguise in the snow-shrouded scenes of the Icy. Interestingly, throughout the late spring, the fur changes to a brown or grayish-earthy colored tone, permitting the fox to mix into the tundra's rough and less cold landscape.

The Icy fox's jacket is made out of a thick underfur and a layer of longer watchman hairs. This mix fills in as a successful separator, assisting the fox with keeping up with its internal heat level in very cool circumstances. Moreover, the fox's short, adjusted ears and a short, stocky gag further diminish heat misfortune.

Cold foxes have advanced a few variations to adapt to the cruel states of their living space. Their fuzzy paws assist them cross the snow and ice effortlessly, and the bottoms of their feet are very much protected, diminishing intensity misfortune. These variations empower them to be dynamic all year in the Icy, regardless of temperatures that can drop well underneath freezing.

Living space and Reach

The Cold fox's reach is circumpolar, meaning it circles the northern districts of the globe. This species can be tracked down in the Icy tundra and waterfront areas of North America, Europe, Asia, and, surprisingly, a few Icy islands. Its reach stretches out from the high Cold to additional mild areas close to the Icy Circle.

Inside this immense region, Cold foxes occupy different scenes, including infertile ice, beach front bluffs, and upland tundra.

Icy foxes are entrepreneurial and flexible in their living space choice. They can be found close to the ocean ice, which furnishes them with admittance to seal bodies and other marine assets. On the tundra, they search out lemming tunnels and other little prey species. Their flexibility is a critical consider their endurance in the difficult Icy climate.

Conduct and Diet

Cold foxes are lone creatures that are regularly dynamic during the nightfall long periods of sunrise and sunset. They have a broad home reach, frequently covering many square miles, looking for food. While they are single commonly, they might frame matches during the reproducing season, from pre-spring to spring early.

One of the essential difficulties of life in the Icy is tying down sufficient food to make due. Cold foxes are omnivores and have a shifted diet that incorporates little well evolved creatures like lemmings, birds, bird eggs, fish, and flesh from bigger hunters, like polar bears and wolves. They are known for their capacity to find and uncover lemming tunnels, making these little rodents a staple in their eating routine throughout the mid year months when it are high to lemming populaces.

Throughout the colder time of year, when food sources become more difficult to find, Icy foxes are known for their rummaging abilities. They will continue in the tracks of bigger hunters like polar bears to devour extras and bodies. Their sharp feeling of smell assists them with finding these food sources in the tremendous and frequently featureless Icy scene.

Variations to Outrageous Circumstances

Getting through in the Icy climate requires a bunch of wonderful variations, and the Cold fox has developed a few methodologies to get through the outrageous circumstances. Its fur, which changes tone with the seasons, gives compelling cover against the snow or rough landscape, assisting it with following prey and dodge hunters.

The fox's conservative body and short legs diminish its surface region, limiting intensity misfortune and preserving energy. The fur on the bottoms of its feet goes about as a warm hindrance, forestalling frostbite. Moreover, the Icy fox has a low metabolic rate, permitting it to make due on moderately low food consumption during the difficult cold weather months.

One of the most entrancing transformations of the Cold fox is its capacity to persevere through freezing temperatures. It can endure temperatures as low as - 70°F (- 57°C) by twisting into a tight ball, tucking its nose under its tail, and involving its cushy tail as an implicit cover. This conduct assists it with preserving body heat and endure the bone chilling Icy evenings.

Multiplication and Everyday Life

Cold foxes are known for their strength in brutal circumstances, and their propagation technique mirrors this durability. They commonly breed in pre-spring or late-winter when the temperatures are still harshly cold. During this time, a mated sets of foxes will lay out a nook, frequently situated in a snowdrift, cliffside cleft, or a tunnel in the ground.

The female Cold fox brings forth a litter of little guys, which can number from one to fourteen, with a normal of six to eight. The puppies are conceived visually impaired and vulnerable, depending on their mom's milk for sustenance. The male regularly helps the female in giving food to the family during this crucial time, assisting with guaranteeing the endurance of the youthful.

As the little guys develop, they go through a lofty expectation to learn and adapt, getting fundamental basic instincts from their folks. They become progressively free and ultimately leave the family nook. Icy foxes arrive at sexual development at about ten months old enough, and they might lay out their own domains and search out mates.

Preservation Status

The preservation status of the Icy fox differs across its reach, yet it faces a few huge difficulties, principally connected with environmental change and human exercises.

Environmental change is making the Cold warm at two times the worldwide normal rate, prompting the deficiency of ocean ice and adjusting the dissemination of prey species. These progressions can influence the accessibility of nourishment for Icy foxes and can likewise prompt expanded rivalry with different hunters like red foxes, which are extending their reach toward the north.

Moreover, expanded human exercises in the Cold, like asset extraction and the travel industry, can adversely affect Icy fox populaces. Living space aggravation and contamination from these exercises can disturb the delicate Cold biological system, further undermining the species.

Protection endeavors are in progress to address these difficulties. These incorporate the assurance of key Cold territories, examination into the species' way of behaving and biology, and checking populaces to all the more likely figure out their elements and necessities. Endeavors are additionally being had to moderate the effects of environmental change on the Icy climate.

6.2 The Mysterious Calls of Arctic Foxes

The Cold fox (Vulpes lagopus) is an enrapturing and baffling animal groups known for its capacity to flourish in the most extreme of conditions, the Icy tundra. While the actual transformations and conduct of these foxes have been irrefutably factual, the vocalizations and specialized strategies for Icy foxes stay a moderately puzzling and under-explored part of their science. In this article, we will dive into the fascinating universe of Cold fox calls, revealing insight into their different vocalizations, their possible capabilities, and the significance of grasping this less popular part of their way of behaving.

The Vocal Collection of Icy Foxes

Icy foxes are not as popular for their vocalizations as some other canid species like wolves or coyotes, yet they really do have a different vocal collection. These vocalizations serve different capabilities all through their lives, from speaking with conspecifics to laying an out area and mating.

Woofing and Howling: Icy foxes frequently bark and howl while cooperating with one another. These shrill vocalizations are usually utilized in friendly settings, like play among little guys or during connections between mates. The woofing and howling can be a method for correspondence inside a family bunch or between adjoining foxes.

Snarling: Snarling is commonly an indication of hostility or advance notice. Cold foxes might snarl when they feel compromised or while protecting their domain or assets. This vocalization fills in as a reasonable sign to different creatures that they ought to ease off.

Crying and Crying: Whining and whimpering are commonly connected with misery, dread, or accommodation. These sounds are in many cases heard in circumstances where a Cold fox is feeling compromised or accommodating to a more predominant person. It might likewise be utilized by puppies to evoke parental consideration and consideration.

Wailing: Yelling is a more uncommon vocalization in Cold foxes contrasted with their bigger cousins, similar to wolves, however it can happen. Yelling might act as a significant distance specialized technique, especially during the reproducing season when mates are looking for one another across tremendous Cold scenes.

Shouting: Icy foxes are known to make penetrating, shocking shouts, especially during the reproducing season. These shouts can be heard reverberating across the tundra and are frequently connected with mating and regional questions.

The Elements of Icy Fox Vocalizations

While the exact elements of Icy fox vocalizations are as yet a subject of progressing research, a few key jobs have been proposed for these calls:

Correspondence inside Family Gatherings: Icy foxes are known to be monogamous and may frame family bunches during the reproducing season. Vocalizations like yelping, howling, and whimpering are probable utilized for correspondence inside these gatherings, assisting with keeping up with social bonds and direction exercises, like hunting and raising puppies.

Regional Protection: The snarls and shouts of Icy foxes are frequently connected with regional debates. These calls might lay out and protect regions, particularly during the rearing season when rivalry for assets and mates is high.

Mating and Fascination: Shouts, wails, and different vocalizations are frequently connected with mating conduct. These calls might act as a way for possible mates to find each other across the huge and frequently featureless Cold scene.

Parent-Posterity Correspondence: Crying and whimpering vocalizations from puppies probably assume a critical part in parent-posterity correspondence. These calls might flag yearning, inconvenience, or a requirement for consideration, guaranteeing that the guardians know about their puppies' necessities.

Hunter Evasion: While not too reported, a few vocalizations, like snarling, may act as an obstacle to expected hunters, making them aware of the presence of the Cold fox and deterring them from drawing nearer.

Challenges in Concentrating on Icy Fox Calls

Concentrating on the vocalizations of Cold foxes presents a few difficulties. First and foremost, their remote and unforgiving living space, combined with the subtle idea of the species, makes it hard to notice them intently in nature. Cold foxes are frequently careful about human presence, and scientists should utilize painless strategies, like distant cameras and acoustic recording gadgets, to catch their vocalizations.

Also, the Icy climate itself can be a deterrent. Cruel weather patterns, including outrageous cold and successive blizzards, can restrict the capacity to direct hands on work and accumulate information. The tremendous scopes of the Icy additionally make it trying to track and screen individual foxes.

Moreover, the cryptic idea of Cold foxes, especially during the rearing season, implies that quite a bit of their vocal way of behaving may slip by everyone's notice or undocumented. This features the requirement for more thorough examination endeavors to reveal the full degree of their vocal collection and the settings where these calls are utilized.

The Transformative Meaning of Icy Fox Vocalizations

The vocalizations of Icy foxes have likely developed as variations to the novel difficulties they face in their current circumstance. Residing in a huge, treeless scene where perceivability is in many cases restricted by snow and ice, sound turns into a crucial method for correspondence. Icy foxes might utilize vocalizations to keep up with social attachment inside family gatherings, track down mates, and safeguard their regions.

Notwithstanding their social and biological capabilities, these calls might have advanced to alleviate clashes and diminish the requirement for actual showdowns. By conveying their goals, sentiments, and status through vocalizations, Icy foxes can keep away from superfluous dangers and wounds.

Understanding the vocal way of behaving of Icy foxes can likewise reveal insight into their transformative history and associations with other canid species. Relative investigations of vocalizations among various canids can assist us with disentangling the transformative history of these species and give bits of knowledge into their common family line and different variations.

Preservation Suggestions

Similarly as with any natural life species, understanding the vocalizations and correspondence of Cold foxes isn't simply a scholarly activity however has pragmatic preservation suggestions.

The Cold climate, whereupon Icy foxes depend, is quickly changing because of environmental change, and their endurance is compromised by moving biological systems and the infringement of additional forceful species, like red foxes.

Endeavors to study and safeguard Cold fox populaces can be improved by an extensive comprehension of their vocal way of behaving.

Observing changes in vocalizations after some time might assist specialists with measuring the effects of ecological changes on the species. Distinguishing explicit calls related with conceptive achievement or regional debates can illuminate designated preservation techniques to safeguard fundamental rearing regions and diminish human aggravation during delicate periods.

6.3 The Adaptations of Arctic Foxes

The Cold fox (Vulpes lagopus) is a little yet diligent vertebrate that calls the bone chilling Icy tundra home. It has developed a surprising set-up of transformations to make due in perhaps of the most unfriendly climate on The planet. From its thick fur and occasional variety change to its particular hunting strategies and low metabolic rate, the Cold fox's transformations are a demonstration of the force of normal choice. In this article, we will investigate the diverse transformations that empower these strong creatures to flourish in the outrageous states of the Icy.

Actual Variations

Thick Protecting Fur: The most famous transformation of the Cold fox is its rich, thick fur. This fur fills in as a powerful protector, keeping the fox warm in outrageous virus. The coat comprises of two layers: a thick, delicate underfur near the skin and longer, watch hairs on the outside. Throughout the colder time of year, the fur turns unadulterated white, giving superb cover against the snow. In the late spring, the fur movements to brown or dark, permitting the fox to mix into the rough and less frigid territory.

Diminished Surface Region: Icy foxes have moderately little bodies, estimating around 18 to 27 inches (46 to 68 centimeters) long, with an extra 11 to 21 inches (28 to 53 centimeters) added by their ragged tails. Their conservative size lessens their surface region, limiting intensity misfortune and making them more dexterous in the snow.

Protected Paws: Icy foxes have shaggy paws that give protection and permit them to move easily on snow and ice. These protecting cushions additionally assist with forestalling frostbite, guaranteeing their feet stay practical in the coldest temperatures.

Short Ears and Gag: The fox's short, adjusted ears and short, stocky gag lessen heat misfortune. This variation is significant for keeping up with internal heat level in very chilly circumstances.

Cushy Tail: The Icy fox's rugged tail isn't simply an improving component; it fills a pragmatic need. At the point when the fox twists up in a tight ball to preserve warmth during the cold Icy evenings, its tail folds over its body, going about as an implicit cover.

Physiological Variations

Low Metabolic Rate: One of the vital physiological variations of the Icy fox is its low metabolic rate. This implies they require less energy to keep up with their physical processes contrasted with numerous different warm blooded animals of their size. A diminished metabolic rate permits them to make due on generally low food consumption, which is imperative in the Icy's unforgiving climate.

Food Capacity Systems: Cold foxes can store food during seasons of overflow by covering it in the ground. This way of behaving, known as reserving, guarantees a consistent food supply during times of shortage. The capacity to recover reserved food when required is a significant step by step process for surviving.

Capacity to Enter Lethargy: During the most brutal cold weather months when food is scant, Icy foxes can enter a condition of slowness, like hibernation. Lethargy permits them to monitor energy by dialing back their metabolic cycles and diminishing their requirement for food.

Effective Stomach related Framework: Icy foxes have a stomach related framework appropriate for their principally meat eating diet. Their short gastrointestinal system considers effective handling of high-protein food sources, which are fundamental for keeping up with energy levels in the cool Cold climate.

Social Variations

Single Way of life: Cold foxes are by and large lone creatures. This social variation lessens rivalry for restricted assets in their cruel environment. Be that as it may, they might frame matches during the rearing season.

Broad Home Reaches: To find food in the huge Icy scene, Cold foxes have broad home ranges that can traverse many square miles. These huge domains permit them to find prey and adjust to changing food accessibility.

Roaming Conduct: Cold foxes are itinerant in their quest for food. They follow their prey and travel impressive distances to find food sources, which is vital in a climate where assets are much of the time spread out.

Hunting Techniques: Cold foxes utilize a scope of hunting methodologies, including following, rummaging, and digging. They are gifted at finding little warm blooded animals like lemmings and other prey, depending on their sharp feeling of smell and hearing to do as such.

Parent-Posterity Correspondence: Parent Cold foxes speak with their little guys through vocalizations, preparing, and actual contact. This assists the youthful foxes with mastering basic instincts and guarantees their prosperity.

Variations for Cold Environments

The variations of Cold foxes are finely tuned to the outrageous states of their current circumstance:

Temperature Limits: The Cold fox's variations are fundamental for getting through temperatures that can plunge to as low as - 70°F (- 57°C). Their thick fur, minimal body, and capacity to twist up and involve their tail as protection all add to their endurance in these outrageous temperatures.

Blanketed and Cold Territory: Icy foxes explore frigid and frosty landscape effortlessly because of their protected paws and short legs, which assist with lessening the gamble of frostbite and make them nimble in the snow.

Restricted Food Assets: The infertile Cold scene offers restricted food assets. Cold foxes have adjusted to this test by being entrepreneurial trackers and foragers, permitting them to change their eating regimen in light of the accessibility of prey.

Absence of Vegetation: Icy foxes frequently use snow tunnels and rock hole as safe house since the desolate Cold scene needs appropriate vegetation for building sanctums.

Traveling Conduct: The migrant way of life of Cold foxes permits them to follow prey, for example, lemmings, whose populaces can vacillate consistently. This versatility guarantees they can find food even in unusual conditions.

Preservation Suggestions

Understanding the variations of Icy foxes is basic for their preservation, particularly notwithstanding environmental change and human exercises that undermine their delicate territory. Environmental change is quickly changing the Cold, prompting shifts in prey accessibility, expanded contest with growing red fox populaces, and territory disturbance. Preservation endeavors should focus on the assurance of key Icy natural surroundings, the decrease of human aggravation in delicate regions, and the observing of Icy fox populaces to guarantee their endurance.

6.4 An Arctic Fox-inspired Lullaby

Settled in the cold scenes of the Icy, where the bone chilling breezes clear across vast tundras and the snow-clad world is a material of unblemished white, the versatile and captivating Icy fox rules. These subtle animals, enhanced in their unblemished white coats and agile in their developments, encapsulate the exceptional versatility expected to make due in one of the World's cruelest surroundings. Amidst this unforgiving wild, the Cold fox arises as an image of the district's getting through magnificence and the intriguing dance of life and nature. The "Icy Fox-roused Bedtime song" winds around an expressive story that praises the soul of these phenomenal animals, catches the cryptic appeal of the Cold, and conveys the calming quintessence of a cradlesong. This melodic excursion conveys us into the core of the Icy's far off wonderland, where life's cadence is a fragile harmony between endurance and serenity.

The Icy is a domain of obvious differences, where severe virus wins, and nature's powers significantly mold existence with a firm hand. Here, the Cold fox, with its perfect white fur, is a paragon of nature's cunning plan. The fox's variation to this unforgiving climate is absolutely surprising, as it changes its jacket's tone to mix flawlessly with the moving seasons, displaying the significance of strength and adaptability despite difficulty. The initial refrains of our bedtime song praise the Icy fox's versatility, passing on the message that, similar to these surprising animals, we also can embrace change and persevere through life's difficulties with beauty.

Underneath the heavenly performance center of Aurora Borealis, the Cold fox sets out on its quiet chase, exploring the tremendous territory of snow with beauty and accuracy. The children's song's tune reflects the fox's strides, summoning the delicate beat of the Icy night's pulse. The entrancing dance of Aurora Borealis paints an ethereal dreamscape above, and the cradlesong's verses welcome us to participate in the sorcery and miracle of this distant world. It transports us to a spot where nature and mystery join, similar as the Cold fox's presence, where the everyday changes into something uncommon underneath the gleaming auroras.

As the Cold night extends on, the bedtime song ushers us more profound into the core of this unblemished wild. It illustrates the Icy's isolation and excellence, where the world is shrouded in shades of white and blue, and the main sounds are the murmurs of the breeze and the far off calls of Icy animals. It urges us to enjoy the serenity that nature's calm minutes offer and the harmony that envelopes us, similar as the Cold fox during its single investigations.

Progressing through the cradlesong, the Icy fox's excursion through the seasons shows signs of life, reflecting the consistently changing excellence of the actual Icy. Similarly as the fox adjusts to the moving scene, the cradlesong's song advances, catching the unique idea of the locale. It fills in as an update that change is a natural piece of life, and, like the Icy fox, we can track down satisfaction in embracing the various times of our reality.

In the core of the Cold, the bedtime song gives recognition to the profound family bonds that exist among these versatile animals. Icy foxes are known for their affectionate nuclear families, and the cradlesong's chorale repeats the glow and love that families give, no matter what the difficulties in the rest of the world. It helps us to remember the meaning of association and backing, conveying a message of affection and solace that the children's song conveys.

As the bedtime song moves toward its decision, it flawlessly winds around together this multitude of components: the versatility of the Cold fox, the charm of Aurora Borealis, the significance of genius, the excellence of isolation, the always evolving seasons, and the strength of family. It makes an agreeable mix of nature's lessons and the unflinching soul of the Icy, typified in a tune that relieves and comforts, satisfying the genuine motivation behind a cradlesong.

In the last notes of the children's song, the Cold fox, with its effortlessness and excellence, turns into an image of trust and motivation. It advises us that even in the cruelest of conditions, life can prosper and flourish. It urges us to adjust, see as wizardry in the standard, be creative, embrace change, and love the obligations of family. The Icy fox's children's song is an update that, similar to the actual fox, we also can explore life's difficulties with effortlessness and flexibility, tracking down magnificence and miracle in the most startling spots.

Chapter 7

The Seal's Slumber Song

In the secret corners of the world, where land and ocean meet in an agreeable dance, a wonderful animal, the seal, views as its home. These delicate marine warm blooded creatures, with their heartfelt eyes and effortless developments, occupy a world that is both charming and secretive. Their lives are a demonstration of the sea's hug and the tranquility of the waterfront domains. This account digs into the core of the seal's presence, as motivated by the ocean and the mitigating cradlesong that reverberates inside the rhythms of their reality. "The Seal's Sleep Tune" is a melodious excursion that praises the soul of these unprecedented creatures, catches the otherworldly appeal of the ocean, and conveys the calming substance of a cradlesong. A song conveys us into the core of the beach front wonderland, where life's tune is a fragile harmony between liveliness and serenity.

The Captivated Seaside Domain

At the convergence of land and ocean lies a mysterious world, where waves kiss the shore and the tides recurring pattern in a ceaseless hug. The seaside domain, a position of peaceful magnificence and untamed miracle, is where the seals track down their safe-haven. These marine warm blooded animals, outfitted with smooth bodies and sharp senses, are impeccably adjusted to explore the unique climate where the earth meets the ocean. Their reality is one of vast skylines, where the musicality of the sea sets the rhythm for their lives. Here, in the midst of the salt-touched air and the ensemble of seabirds, we start our investigation of "The Seal's Sleep Tune."

The Marks of the Ocean

Seals, with their different species and exceptional transformations, are a demonstration of the wondrous variety of marine life. From the magnificent elephant seals that standard over the rough sea shores to the energetic harbor seals that loll in the sun, every species has an extraordinary story to tell. We dive into the existences of these charming animals, finding out about their ways of behaving, environments, and the natural importance they hold in the waterfront biological systems. Through their encounters, we gain a more profound appreciation for the concordance that exists in the beach front domains and the unpredictable jobs that seals play inside this sensitive equilibrium.

The Ocean's Children's song

The ocean has its own cradlesong, a hypnotizing orchestra of waves and tides that calms the spirit. In this part, we investigate the relieving characteristics of the ocean, ageless melody addresses the hearts of all who tune in. The rhythmic movement of the tides, the delicate lap of waves against the shore, and the far off calls of seabirds make a quiet song that wraps the beach front domain. We uncover the secrets of the ocean's cradlesong and the way in which it resounds in the existences of seals, quieting their spirits and directing them through the consistently evolving waters.

The Dance of Fun loving nature

Seals are prestigious for their perky nature, and their seaside jungle gyms are fields of joy. With deft bodies and curious personalities, seals take part in a charming dance of energy. We investigate the tricks of seal puppies as they skip in the surf, the synchronized developments of seals at play, and the energetic cooperations between these marine creatures.

Their fun loving attitude helps us to remember the significance of bliss and extravagance, even in the most unusual of conditions.

The Quietness of Sleep

In the midst of the wonder of the waterfront world and the perkiness of seal life, there lies a snapshot of perfect serenity — the seal's sleep. Seals are experts of rest and unwinding, looking for comfort on rough outcrops and sandy shores. Their peaceful rest is an impression of the ocean's calming embrace, a supportive sleep that recharges their spirits for the undertakings that lie ahead. This section investigates the craft of seal sleep, how they track down wellbeing and quietness in the beach front domain, and the fantasies that might clear them away to the profundities of the sea.

The Preservation Orchestra

The charm of the waterfront domain and the excellence of the seal's presence are not without their difficulties. In this part, we dive into the preservation endeavors and the need to safeguard the territories and lives of these amazing marine vertebrates. The delicate equilibrium of beach front biological systems, the dangers that seals face, and the actions being taken to guarantee their endurance are all essential for the preservation orchestra. Through training and activity, we can add to the amicable conjunction of seals and their seaside surroundings.

The Seal's Sleep Tune: A Cradlesong for All

The seal's sleep tune isn't simply a song that resounds inside the existences of seals; a cradlesong for all are moved by its wizardry. We investigate how this cradlesong can be a wellspring of motivation, calming our spirits, and interfacing us with the rhythms of the ocean. As we drench ourselves in the seal's reality, we find the significant association among nature and our own prosperity, drawing examples of serenity, perkiness, and protection that improve our lives.

Reverberations of the Beach front Domain

As our excursion through "The Seal's Sleep Tune" comes to a nearby, we ponder the getting through reverberations of the seaside domain and the existences of seals. The charming dance of the land

and ocean, the bedtime song of the sea, the fun loving nature of seals, and the tranquility of their sleep all leave permanent engravings on our souls. These reverberations help us to remember the magnificence and marvel that exist in the regular world, encouraging us to embrace the beach front domains and the soul of the seals with a newly discovered appreciation.

7.1 Introduction to Arctic Seals

The Icy, a district of outrageous cold and ice, is home to a different cluster of natural life, a considerable lot of which have developed explicit transformations to get by in this brutal climate. Among these animals, the Icy seals are the absolute generally charming. These marine well evolved creatures have adjusted to the chilly, frigid waters and remote scenes, where they assume a urgent part in the Icy environment.

Icy seals have a place with the family Phocidae, which incorporates genuine seals. They are portrayed by their smoothed out bodies, flippers, and an absence of outside ear folds. The Cold climate is a difficult one for any animal categories, and Icy seals have developed a great many variations to flourish in this outrageous setting.

This extensive aide will dig into the scientific categorization and variety of Icy seals, their extraordinary transformations for life in the Icy, their conveyance and natural surroundings, conduct, diet, protection status, and the advancing connections among people and these amazing animals. By investigating these perspectives, we can acquire a more profound enthusiasm for the basic job that Icy seals play in the biological system and the difficulties they face in a quickly changing Icy climate.

Icy Seals: Scientific categorization and Variety

Icy seals, as a feature of the family Phocidae, have a place with the request Pinnipedia. Pinnipeds are a different gathering of marine warm blooded creatures that likewise incorporates ocean lions and walruses. The Icy seal family, Phocidae, contains various species adjusted to cold waters and ice-covered scenes. The most regularly experienced Cold seals include:

Harp Seals (Pagophilus groenlandicus): These seals are known for their unmistakable dark harp-molded markings on their fur. They are all around adjusted to ice-covered conditions and are renowned for their yearly movement.

Ringed Seals (Pusa hispida): Ringed seals are the littlest and most plentiful seals in the Icy. They are named for the light-shaded rings on their fur. These seals are ice subject matter experts, frequently making and keeping up with breathing openings through the ice.

Whiskery Seals (Erignathus barbatus): Hairy seals are enormous, hearty seals with unmistakable fiber like bristles. They basically occupy shallow, ice-shrouded waters and utilize areas of strength for them to smash their prey.

Weddell Seals (Leptonychotes weddellii): Albeit principally found in Antarctica, little populaces of Weddell seals possess the Cold. They are known for their uncommonly profound and long jumps.

Hooded Seals (Cystophora cristata): These seals are effectively unmistakable by the huge, inflatable, expand like sacs on their noses. They are ice-related seals, frequently involving ice floes as resting stages.

Walrus (Odobenus rosmarus): While false seals, walruses are a critical piece of the Cold marine warm blooded creature local area. They are known for their long tusks and broad utilization of ocean ice as take out locales.

The variety inside this family mirrors the capacity of seals to adjust to different specialties inside the Cold climate. Every species has own remarkable qualities and transformations make it appropriate to explicit environmental jobs inside this brutal and freezing scene.

Variations to Cold Life

Life in the Icy is testing, described by frigid temperatures, frosty waters, and restricted admittance to food. Icy seals have developed a scope of surprising variations that empower them to flourish in this outrageous climate:

Thick Lard: Icy seals have a thick layer of fat underneath their skin, which fills in as protection against the cold and gives an energy hold during times of fasting.

Smoothed out Bodies: Their bodies are smoothed out for proficient swimming, permitting them to explore through cold waters with insignificant obstruction.

Webbed Flippers: Seals have webbed flippers that assist them with moving nimbly in the water and increment their swimming effectiveness.

Warm Countercurrent Framework: These seals have an extraordinary circulatory framework that keeps indispensable organs warm while permitting their limits to cool. This limits heat misfortune in cool water.

Low Metabolic Rates: Icy seals have low metabolic rates, empowering them to moderate energy during long jumps and times of fasting.

Ice Transformations: A few animal categories, as ringed seals, are ice subject matter experts. They have solid hooks to keep up with breathing openings through thick ice and utilize these openings to conceive an offspring and access food.

Fat Digestion: An Icy seals can change the sythesis of their fat to adjust to occasional varieties in diet and energy prerequisites.

Profound Jumping skills: Species like the Weddell seals are prestigious for their remarkable plunging capacities, with the capacity to arrive at shocking profundities while scrounging.

These variations permit Icy seals to get by as well as flourish in a district where most different creatures would battle to exist.

Environment and Conveyance

Cold seals are transcendently found in the circumpolar Icy district, which incorporates the Icy Sea and its fringe oceans, as well as the encompassing bodies of land. They are profoundly specific for life around here and are firmly connected with ocean ice, which assumes a crucial part in their environment.

The conveyance of Cold seals is impacted by the degree and thickness of ocean ice, which fluctuates occasionally. A few seals, like the ringed seals, are ice-related and depend on the ice for rearing, shedding, and resting. Conversely, species like the hairy seals are more adaptable in their territory prerequisites and can be found in both ice-shrouded and without ice waters.

Living space choice is affected by a few elements, including:

Reproducing and Pupping Locales: Icy seals bring forth their young on ocean ice, where little guys are protected from hunters and can get to breathing openings for endurance.

Searching Living space: Seals expect admittance to breathing openings and leads in the ice to scrounge for their favored prey, like fish and spineless creatures.

Shedding Areas: Seals shed every year, and during this time, they frequently pull out onto ice floes or islands to shed their old fur.

Resting Destinations: Ice floes and stable ice highlights give urgent resting locales to seals to moderate energy.

The conveyance of Cold seals isn't just affected by regular factors yet in addition by anthropogenic exercises and environmental change, which are essentially adjusting their natural surroundings. The quick decrease of ocean ice because of an unnatural weather change represents an extreme danger to these species, driving them to adjust to new circumstances or face the gamble of decline.

Conduct and Life History

Icy seals show a scope of ways of behaving that are fundamental for their endurance and regenerative achievement. Understanding their way of behaving and life history is urgent for their protection and biological comprehension:

Rearing and Pupping: Cold seals bring forth their little guys on the ice, where they are protected from hunters. Female seals quick during this time, depending on their lard stores to sustain their posterity.

Shedding: Seals shed one time each year, shedding their old fur. Shedding is a basic period when seals are many times seen pulled out on ice floes.

Scrounging and Plunging: Icy seals are gifted jumpers, equipped for arriving at great profundities to chase after prey. They frequently use breaks in the ice as passageways for rummaging.

Regional Way of behaving: A few seals, like the whiskery seal, are known to display regional way of behaving, protecting their favored scrounging regions.

Social Design: While not quite as gregarious as ocean lions, Icy seals can shape free gatherings, particularly during the rearing season.

Movement: A few animal categories, similar to harp seals, embrace significant distance relocations to track down food and reproducing destinations. Their movements can be impacted by the moving ice designs because of environmental change.

Vocalizations: Seals convey utilizing different vocalizations, like submerged calls, to keep up with social securities and impart submerged.

The existence history of Cold seals is intently attached to the yearly patterns of ocean ice development and liquefy. As environmental change modifies these cycles, it can possibly upset the planning of basic life altering situations, influencing the general wellbeing and endurance of seal populaces.

Diet and Taking care of Procedures

Cold seals are shrewd hunters, going after various marine species that are accessible in their current circumstance. Their eating regimens can fluctuate by species and area, however the most widely recognized prey things for Cold seals include:

Fish: Numerous Icy seals feed on an assortment of fish animal types, including Icy cod and herring. These fish are significant wellsprings of energy for seals.

Spineless creatures: Seals additionally consume spineless creatures like shrimp, squid, and different types of scavangers.

Tiny fish: Youthful seals, specifically, may benefit from zooplankton, which can be bountiful in a few Cold waters.

Benthic Species: A few seals, as hairy seals, have adjusted to benefit from benthic species found on the ocean bottom. They utilize areas of strength for them to squash shellfish and other prey.

Dominant hunters: Bigger seals, similar to the panther seal, are known to go after different seals, especially little guys.

Icy seals are gifted trackers and utilize their smoothed out bodies, sharp teeth, and solid jaws to get and consume their prey. Their eating regimen frequently changes with the season, as they exploit the accessibility of various prey things. These taking care of procedures are finely tuned to the natural elements of the Icy marine climate.

Human Collaborations and Exploration

Cold seals have for some time been essential to native Icy people group as a wellspring of food, dress, and materials for customary instruments. In certain areas, hunting seals is as yet a fundamental piece of the social and monetary texture. Nonetheless, the connection among people and Cold seals has developed with evolving times.

Conventional Hunting: Native people groups in the Icy have a long history of seal hunting. These chases are frequently directed economically, with a profound regard for the creatures and their current circumstance.

Business Hunting: Business seal hunting has been a hostile issue, especially when directed impractically. Numerous nations have forced guidelines to safeguard seal populaces.

The travel industry: Cold the travel industry is on the ascent, and seal-watching has turned into a well known fascination. Nonetheless, dependable the travel industry is fundamental to try not to upset seals and their environments.

Research: Logical exploration on Cold seals is essential for figuring out their biology, conduct, and the effects of environmental change. This examination frequently includes labeling seals, checking their developments, and concentrating on their physiology.

Preservation Endeavors: Associations and states are attempting to safeguard seal populaces and their environments. This incorporates the foundation of marine safeguarded regions and the advancement of preservation plans.

Human connections with Cold seals are turning out to be progressively complicated as environmental change and business intrigues drive changes in the Icy. Feasible administration and protection endeavors are essential to guarantee the proceeded with endurance of these striking creatures.

7.2 The Haunting Songs of Seals

Seals, frequently connected with the cold waters of the world's seas, are known for their particular and frightful vocalizations that convey across the oceans. These unpleasant tunes of seals have charmed the human creative mind for a really long time, motivating old stories, fantasies, and logical exploration. In this investigation, we will dig into the hypnotizing universe of seal vocalizations, uncovering the different species that produce these sounds, their motivations, and the entrancing exploration that keeps on unwinding the secrets of their melodies.

1. **The Confounding Universe of Seal Vocalizations**

   Seals have a place with the request Pinnipedia, which incorporates three principal families: Phocidae (genuine seals), Otariidae (eared seals, for example, ocean lions and fur seals), and Odobenidae (walruses). While eared seals are frequently known for their uproarious thunders and calls, genuine seals, which have no outside ear folds, are the essential center with regards to baffling seal melodies. The vocalizations of genuine seals are frequently depicted as tormenting because of their powerful, creepy quality.

2. **Species that Sing**

   A few types of genuine seals are known for their vocalizations. Outstanding models include:

   Weddell Seals (Leptonychotes weddellii): These seals, fundamentally tracked down in Antarctica, are known for their charming and complex tunes. Weddell seals produce a progression of quavers and trills during submerged correspondence.

Weddell Seals (Leptonychotes weddellii): These seals, essentially tracked down in Antarctica, are known for their charming and complex melodies. Weddell seals produce a progression of quavers and tweets during submerged correspondence.

Dark Seals (Halichoerus grypus): Dim seals, normally saw as in the North Atlantic, are known for their profound, melancholy calls that convey for significant distances.

Harp Seals (Pagophilus groenlandicus): Harp seals produce various shocking calls, including "banshee moans," which are reminiscent of spooky cries and are utilized in friendly and conceptive settings.

Weddell Seals (Leptonychotes weddellii): These seals, fundamentally tracked down in Antarctica, are known for their charming and complex tunes. Weddell seals produce a progression of quavers and peeps during submerged correspondence.

Ringed Seals (Pusa hispida): While not too known for their vocalizations, ringed seals are known to create sharp, ghostly calls that are significant for correspondence during the reproducing season.

These seals utilize their tunes for different purposes, including mate fascination, domain foundation, and correspondence with their puppies.

3. **The Motivation behind Seal Melodies**

Seal vocalizations fill various needs in their lives, and the cryptic tunes of these marine vertebrates are a long way from simple commotion. The basic roles of seal tunes include:

1. **Mate Fascination and Correspondence**
   Seal melodies assume a critical part in mate fascination and match

holding. Male seals frequently utilize their vocalizations to charm females, flagging their wellness and availability to mate. Females, thusly, answer the tunes of guys, flagging their openness.

2. **Region Foundation**

   In certain species, similar to dark seals, melodies are a likewise used to lay out area and protect it from rival guys. These regional calls are in many cases profound, full, and intended to threaten possible challengers.

3. **Mother-Little guy Correspondence**

   Seal moms speak with their puppies through vocalizations. These calls assist puppies with finding their moms on jam-packed ice floes and are urgent for their endurance. Unmistakable calls are utilized to lay out individual characters.

4. **Social Communication**

Seals are not single creatures; they frequently assemble in bunches during rearing and shedding seasons. Vocalizations are fundamental for social communication inside these get-togethers, keeping up with bunch attachment and order.

4. The Study of Seal Melodies

Logical comprehension of seal vocalizations has progressed significantly lately, on account of mechanical headways. Scientists utilize submerged mouthpieces, known as hydrophones, to record seal melodies and investigate their acoustic properties. These examinations have uncovered charming experiences into the design and capability of these unpleasant tunes.

One critical revelation is that seal melodies are profoundly individualistic. Very much like human voices, each seal has a novel vocal mark. This uniqueness is fundamental for mother-little guy acknowledgment and for seals to recognize possible mates or adversaries.

Moreover, the intricacy of seal melodies has been a subject of interest. While certain tunes are moderately straightforward, others, similar to those of Weddell seals, show mind boggling designs and are remembered to pass on more data than recently accepted. Scientists are as yet attempting to translate the implications behind these mind boggling tunes.

5. The Social Meaning of Seal Tunes

Seal melodies have long held social importance in different native networks living in seal-rich districts. Inuit and other Cold native people groups, for instance, have a profound social association with seals and their melodies. These melodies are integrated into conventional functions, narrating, and social practices. They serve as a wellspring of motivation as well as a method for passing down information starting with one age then onto the next.

Seal melodies are much of the time seen as a scaffold between the human and creature universes, stressing the interconnectedness of every single living being. They are a sign of the significant connection between native people groups and the creatures that support them.

6. Dangers to Seal Melodies

While seal melodies have continued for a really long time, they are confronting new difficulties in the cutting edge world. Environmental change, modern exercises, and territory debasement are influencing the way of behaving and endurance of seal populaces. These progressions can likewise affect their vocalizations:

Loss of Natural surroundings: Contracting ocean ice because of an Earth-wide temperature boost can disturb the reproducing and shedding propensities for seals, possibly influencing the specific situation and timing of their tunes.

Human Commotion Contamination: Expanded transportation and modern exercises in the Cold can prompt clamor contamination that upsets seal conduct and correspondence. The many-sided melodies of seals can be overwhelmed by the persevering commotion of human action.

Overfishing: Overfishing of the seals' prey can prompt lack of healthy sustenance and populace declines, which can, thusly, influence their vocalizations.

7. The Eventual fate of Seal Tunes

The eerie tunes of seals are a demonstration of the rich embroidery of life on the planet's seas. They are a sign of the intricacy and excellence of the marine climate and the interconnectedness of all species that call it home. Understanding and protecting these melodies isn't just pivotal for logical examination yet additionally for social legacy and the safeguarding of the environments in which seals assume a crucial part.

Endeavors to safeguard seal populaces, manage human exercises in their environments, and battle environmental change are fundamental to guarantee that the frightful tunes of seals keep on reverberating across the seas. As innovation progresses and our comprehension of these melodies develops, we might open much more mysteries of their motivation and importance in the existences of these confounding marine vertebrates.

7.3 The Diversity of Seal Species in the Arctic

1. **Presentation**

   The Icy, with its immense stretches of ice and testing conditions, fills in as a basic territory for a wide cluster of natural life. Among the most notable occupants of this district are the seals. Cold seals have a place with the family Phocidae, known as evident seals, and have adjusted to life in the bone chilling waters of the Icy Sea and its fringe oceans. They are momentous animals, each with own extraordinary attributes and variations empower them to flourish in this outrageous setting.

2. **Scientific classification of Cold Seals**

Understanding the variety of Icy seals starts with their scientific categorization. These seals are individuals from the request Pinnipedia, a gathering of marine vertebrates described by their semi-sea-going way of life. Inside Pinnipedia, there are three fundamental families:

Phocidae (Genuine Seals): These are the most various group of seals and are described by their absence of outer ear folds and their smoothed out bodies. Most of Icy seals have a place with this family.

Odobenidae (Walruses): While walruses are false seals, they are a critical piece of the Cold marine warm blooded creature local area. They are known for their long tusks and broad utilization of ocean ice as take out locales.

Otariidae (Eared Seals): Eared seals, including ocean lions and fur seals, are fundamentally tracked down in the sub-Icy districts and are known for their outer ear folds and more earthbound ways of behaving.

The family Phocidae, or genuine seals, contains a scope of animal categories adjusted to life in chilly waters and ice-covered scenes. Coming up next are a portion of the eminent Icy seal species:

1. **Harp Seals (Pagophilus groenlandicus)**

   Harp seals are known for their striking appearance, with dark harp-molded markings on their fur. They are all around adjusted to ice-covered conditions and are renowned for their yearly relocation, during which they bring forth and attendant their little guys on the ice.

2. **Ringed Seals (Pusa hispida)**

   Ringed seals are the littlest and most bountiful seals in the Cold. They are named for the light-hued rings on their fur. These seals are ice trained professionals, frequently making and keeping up with breathing openings through the ice, which they use for admittance to the water, rearing, and pupping.

3. **Whiskery Seals (Erignathus barbatus)**

   Whiskery seals are enormous, strong seals with particular fiber like hairs. They essentially possess shallow, ice-shrouded waters and utilize areas of strength for them to pulverize their prey, like shellfishes and other benthic species.

4. **Weddell Seals (Leptonychotes weddellii)**

   While principally found in Antarctica, little populaces of Weddell seals occupy the Icy. They are known for their particularly profound and long plunges, which are critical for searching.

5. **Hooded Seals (Cystophora cristata)**

Hooded seals are effectively conspicuous by the enormous, inflatable, expand like sacs on their noses. They are ice-related seals, frequently involving ice floes as resting stages during reproducing and shedding.

3. Transformations to Icy Life

Getting through in the Icy is quite difficult, and Icy seals have developed a scope of noteworthy variations to assist them with flourishing in this difficult climate:

1. **Thick Lard**

   Icy seals have a thick layer of lard underneath their skin, which fills in as protection against the cold and gives an energy hold during times of fasting.

2. **Smoothed out Bodies**

   Their bodies are smoothed out for productive swimming, permitting them to explore through frosty waters with insignificant obstruction.

3. **Webbed Flippers**

   Seals have webbed flippers that assist them with moving effortlessly in the water and increment their swimming effectiveness.

4. **Warm Countercurrent Framework**

   These seals have an extraordinary circulatory framework that keeps indispensable organs warm while permitting their limits to cool. This limits heat misfortune in cool water.

5. **Low Metabolic Rates**

   Icy seals have low metabolic rates, empowering them to save energy during long jumps and times of fasting.

6. **Ice Variations**

   A few animal types, as ringed seals, are ice subject matter experts. They have solid hooks to keep up with breathing openings through thick ice and utilize these openings to conceive an off-spring, nurture their puppies, and access their prey.

7. **Fat Digestion**

A Cold seals can change the piece of their lard to adjust to occasional varieties in diet and energy prerequisites.

8. **Profound Plunging skills**

Species like the Weddell seals are prestigious for their uncommon jumping capacities, with the capacity to arrive at amazing profundities while scrounging.

These transformations permit Cold seals to get by as well as flourish in a district where most different creatures would battle to exist.

4. Living space and Dissemination

The dispersion of Cold seals is impacted by the degree and thickness of ocean ice, which shifts occasionally. While they are fundamentally found in the Icy Sea and its fringe oceans, every species has its own living space inclinations and variations:

1. **Rearing and Pupping Destinations**

   Icy seals bring forth their young on ocean ice, where puppies are protected from hunters and can get to breathing openings for endurance.

2. **Scavenging Territory**

   Seals expect admittance to breathing openings and leads in the ice to scavenge for their favored prey, like fish, spineless creatures, and tiny fish.

3. **Shedding Areas**

   Seals shed yearly, and during this time, they frequently pull out onto ice floes or islands to shed their old fur and develop new pelage.

4. **Resting Destinations**

Ice floes and stable ice highlights give significant resting locales to seals to moderate energy and departure the cold waters.

The appropriation of Cold seals isn't just impacted by normal factors yet additionally by anthropogenic exercises and environmental change, which are altogether adjusting their natural surroundings. The fast decrease of ocean ice because of an Earth-wide temperature boost represents an extreme danger to these species, constraining them to adjust to new circumstances or face the gamble of decline.

5. Conduct and Life History

Icy seals display a scope of ways of behaving that are fundamental for their endurance and regenerative achievement:

1. **Rearing and Pupping**

   Icy seals bring forth their little guys on the ice, where they are protected from hunters. Female seals quick during this time, depending on their lard stores to support their posterity.

2. **Shedding**

   Seals shed one time per year, shedding their old fur and developing new pelage. Shedding is a basic period when seals are many times seen pulled out on ice floes.

3. **Rummaging and Jumping**

   Cold seals are talented jumpers, fit for arriving at amazing profundities to chase after prey. They frequently use breaks in the ice as passages for scrounging.

4. **Regional Way of behaving**

   A few seals, like hairy seals, are known to show regional way of behaving, protecting their favored scavenging regions.

5. **Social Construction**

   While not so gregarious as ocean lions, Icy seals can frame free gatherings, particularly during the reproducing season. These gatherings are fundamental for correspondence, mating, and security.

6. Movement

A few animal types, similar to harp seals, embrace significant distance relocations to track down food and reproducing destinations. Their relocations can be impacted by the moving ice designs because of environmental change.

7. Vocalizations

Seals impart utilizing different vocalizations, like submerged calls, to keep up with social securities and convey submerged.

The existence history of Cold seals is intently attached to the yearly patterns of ocean ice development and dissolve. As environmental change adjusts these cycles, it can possibly upset the planning of basic life altering situations, influencing the general wellbeing and endurance of seal populaces.

6. Diet and Taking care of Procedures

Cold seals are deft hunters, going after different marine species that are accessible in their current circumstance. Their eating regimens can fluctuate by species and area, yet the most well-known prey things for Icy seals include:

1. Fish

Numerous Icy seals feed on an assortment of fish animal varieties, including Cold cod and herring. These fish are significant wellsprings of energy for seals.

2. Spineless creatures

Seals additionally consume spineless creatures like shrimp, squid, and different types of shellfish.

3. Microscopic fish

Youthful seals, specifically, may benefit from zooplankton, which can be plentiful in a few Cold waters.

4. Benthic Species

A few seals, as hairy seals, have adjusted to benefit from benthic species found on the ocean bottom. They utilize serious areas of strength for them to smash shellfish and other prey.

5. Dominant hunters

Bigger seals, similar to the panther seal, are known to go after different seals, especially little guys.

Icy seals are talented trackers and utilize their smoothed out bodies, sharp teeth, and solid jaws to get and consume their prey. Their eating routine frequently shifts with the season, as they exploit the accessibility of various prey things. These taking care of techniques are finely tuned to the natural elements of the Cold marine climate.

7. The Fate of Cold Seals

The variety of seal species in the Icy addresses a crucial part of the district's environment. These striking animals have adjusted to life in perhaps of the most brutal climate on The planet, assuming critical parts in keeping up with the equilibrium of the Cold environment. As the Cold goes through quick ecological changes because of environmental change, the eventual fate of Icy seals is questionable.

To get the fate of these amazing marine warm blooded creatures, it is fundamental for keep exploring their way of behaving, variations, and connections with the changing Cold climate. Preservation endeavors ought to zero in on safeguarding their territories, controlling human exercises, and elevating manageable practices to guarantee that the variety of seal species in the Icy perseveres for a long time into the future.

The account of Cold seals is one of flexibility, variation, and the persevering through association between these amazing animals and their frozen world. By safeguarding the variety of seal species in the Icy, we add to the general wellbeing and equilibrium of the Cold biological system and gain a more profound comprehension of the complicated collaborations inside this one of a kind and delicate climate.

7.4 A Seal-inspired Lullaby

The delicate recurring pattern of the sea, a cradlesong that has entertained humankind for quite a long time. As the waves stroke the shores and the twilight moves upon the water, the ocean offers a mitigating song, a solicitation to the place that is known for dreams. Among the endless animals that call the sea home, the seals, with their perky tricks and tranquil presence, rouse an exceptional children's song that rises above the limits of land and ocean. In this story, we investigate the universe of seals and their impact on a sincere and relieving children's song, associating us to the sorcery of the ocean and its immortal rhythms.

The Sea's Melody

The story starts on a peaceful seaside night, where the sea's delicate mumble pervades the air. Under the shining embroidery of stars, a mother looks at her kid, a delicate heap of interest and honesty. She perceives the requirement for a bedtime song, an immortal custom that meshes solace into the texture of a youngster's childhood. She wants to make a song that will convey her youngster to the profundities of rest, yet she yearns for more than the commonplace cradlesong. She longs for a bedtime song that typifies the power and elegance of the sea, a cradlesong motivated by the seals.

The Captivated Seals

Seals, with their smooth, oceanic elegance and expressive eyes, possess the boundary between two universes. These charming animals have enamored the human creative mind for quite a long time, their double presence in both ocean and land exemplifying the fragile equilibrium of life itself. The mother, with her kid in her arms, leaves on an excursion to uncover the mysteries of the seals, looking for the motivation for the ideal children's song.

Seals are a different gathering of marine vertebrates, every species having one of a kind qualities that add to their unquestionable charm. From the gigantic elephant seals to the perky harbor seals and the subtle panther marks of the Antarctic, these animals navigate the oceans with style and reason. Their unmistakable calls, suggestive of a blend of barks and tunes, are a demonstration of their position in the immense maritime ensemble.

The Dance of the Harbor Seal

The mother and youngster end up on a rough coastline, where the sun paints the skyline in warm tints of orange and pink. In this pure setting, they experience a gathering of harbor seals. These seals are known for their lively nature and dexterity, making them ideal motivations for a cradlesong.

The harbor seals take to the water in a synchronized dance, their bodies moving nimbly underneath the waves. The mother watches in amazement as the seals diversion, their balances making swells on a superficial level. She understands that the seals' developments resemble a dance, a cadenced artful dance of the ocean.

She listens near the sounds they make, an amicable mix of barks and quavers. The mother wonders about how these sounds reverberation the sea's steadily evolving rhythms, an indication of the ocean's timeless hug. She realizes she has found the substance of her seal-motivated bedtime song.

The Tune of the Sea

Back home, the mother starts to form the seal-propelled bedtime song. She sits at her piano, her fingers stroking the keys, looking for the ideal notes to catch the quintessence of the harbor seals' dance. The song that arises is liquid and tranquil, suggestive of the delicate influencing of the sea.

The verses she composes reflect the seals' energetic soul and the sea's ageless charm:

The mother sings the cradlesong to her kid, and as the notes stream, the youngster's eyelids develop weighty, calmed by the relieving tune. It's a demonstration of the force of music, interfacing the human heart to the normal world, and the timeless connection between a mother and her kid.

The Call of the Elephant Seal

As the kid develops, the mother keeps on looking for motivation from the seals. This time, she dares to the rough shores where the huge elephant seals live. These monster animals, with their booming thunders and strong presence, offer a glaring difference to the smooth harbor seals.

The mother looks as two male elephant seals participate in a savage, yet strangely entrancing, fight for strength. Their profound, throaty calls resound through the air, repeating the greatness of the ocean. She understands that even in their monster may, the elephant seals are a demonstration of the sea's crude power.

The Cradlesong of the Profound

Roused by the elephant seals, the mother makes another bedtime song, one that commends the glory and strength of the sea. The tune is profound and thunderous, reflecting the earth-shaking thunders of the elephant seals. The verses mirror the base excellence of the ocean:The mother sings the cradlesong to her youngster, and the kid floats into a profound and tranquil sleep, contacted by the respect for the endless ocean and its grand animals.

The Puzzle of the Panther Seal

Years pass, and the youngster develops into a teen with a profound love for the sea and its animals. At some point, the mother and kid leave on a remarkable experience to the cold regions of Antarctica, looking for the confounding panther seals. These dominant hunters of the Antarctic waters have a quality of secret and peril that enraptures the creative mind.

The mother and kid spot a panther seal relaxing on an ice floe, its mottled coat flickering in the pale Antarctic daylight. Yet again the panther seal's eyes appear to hold the insider facts of the frozen world, and the mother is enlivened to make a cradlesong, this time catching the persona of the panther seals.

The Song of the Panther Seal

Back at home, the mother pens a bedtime song that exemplifies the soul of the panther seals. The song is tormenting and ethereal, suggestive of the frosty breadth of Antarctica. The verses inspire the puzzler of the panther seals and the charm of the frozen wild:The mother sings the bedtime song to her youngster, and the teen is shipped to the cold excellence of Antarctica, where the panther seals rule as gatekeepers of the ice.

A Bond Beyond anything describable

As the youngster turns into a grown-up, the mother's children's songs have turned into a valued piece of their lives. The seal-motivated cradlesongs have woven a profound association among them and the sea. They have found that the universe of seals is an impression of the world inside themselves, a universe of magnificence, strength, and secret.

Passing Down the Cradlesongs

Years after the fact, the kid, presently a parent, conveys the custom of the seal-motivated cradlesongs to their own kid. They acquaint the cutting edge with the marvels of the ocean, sharing accounts of harbor seals moving in the twilight, elephant seals thundering in the profundities, and panther seals tormenting the frozen Antarctic.

Along these lines, the captivating universe of seals keeps on motivating bedtime songs that overcome any issues among land and ocean, associating ages to the immortal rhythms of the sea. The seals, with their effortlessness, power, and secret, have turned into a piece of the family's legacy, an indication of the endless magnificence and sorcery of the ocean.

Chapter 8

The Arctic Owl's Sonata

The Quiet White Wild

The Icy, a place where there is quiet, immaculate whiteness, is a position of obvious excellence and unforgiving brutality. It is where life gets by and flourishes in the most difficult of conditions. In the midst of this frozen field, the Icy owl, with its ethereal presence, arises as an image of both endurance and beauty. In this story, we set out on an excursion into the Cold wild, revealing the mysteries of the Icy owl, and the hauntingly wonderful sonata it winds through the ages.

The Puzzling Cold Owl

The Cold owl, otherwise called the frigid owl, is an animal of mystery. Its unadulterated white plumage permits it to mix flawlessly into the Icy scene, a spooky phantom against the snow and ice. The Icy owl is both an image of virtue and an indication of the privileged insights concealed inside the frozen heart of the North.

These grand birds have caught the human creative mind for quite a long time. They have been loved by the native individuals of the Cold, who accept the owls have the insight of the ages. For scientists and picture takers, the Cold owl stays a slippery and interesting subject.

The Unforgiving Cold Environment

The Icy is a position of limits. Its environment is described by severe chilly, determined breezes, and long stretches of close complete murkiness throughout the colder time of year. In this bone chilling wild, the Icy owl has developed to flourish. It is an expert of endurance, fit for getting through the most extreme of conditions.

The Icy owl's thick plumage and enormous size assist it with holding warmth exposed, while its sharp visual perception and intense hearing make it an effective hunter. Its eating routine fundamentally comprises of lemmings, a little rat that populates the tundra, supporting the owl during the long Cold winters.

The Icy Owl's Frightful Call

One of the most spellbinding parts of the Icy owl is its frightful call. This distressed, repeating sound resounds through the ruined scene, conveying a feeling of isolation and secret. The Inuit nation of the Cold have long connected the owl's call with the spirits of the land, accepting that it conveys messages from the otherworld.

The part dives into the scary, hypnotizing nature of the Cold owl's call and its effect on the human mind. It investigates the notions and legends that have developed around this puzzling bird.

The Cold Owl's Hunting Sonata

The Cold owl's hunting strategies are out and out sensational. With quiet wings, it floats over the tundra, examining the snow-shrouded scene for the smallest development. Its striking secrecy and accuracy in hunting make it one of the top hunters in the Cold environment.

The section follows the owl as it chases, catching the substance of its lone presence. The Icy owl's hunting sonata is an ensemble of tolerance, effortlessness, and lethal productivity. Through its eyes, we witness the delicate equilibrium of life and passing in the brutal Icy climate.

The Cold Owl in Fantasy and Legend

Since forever ago, the Cold owl has held an extraordinary spot in the fantasies and legends of different societies. In Nordic folklore, it is related with shrewdness and direction, frequently portrayed as the friend of the goddess of astuteness, Athena. In native Cold fables, the owl is respected as a courier of the spirits, filling in as an extension between the living and the extraordinary.

This section investigates the rich embroidery of fantasies and legends that have been woven around the Cold owl, featuring its job as an image of secret, insight, and the interconnectedness of every single living thing.

The Cold Owl's Relocations

In spite of the brutality of the Icy, the Icy owl attempts mind blowing movements, heading out a huge number of miles to find food and reasonable settling grounds. The section dives into the exceptional excursion of the owl, investigating the difficulties it faces during its movements and the logical bits of knowledge acquired from following these sublime birds.

The Cold owl's transient way of behaving has fascinated researchers, as they look to disentangle the insider facts of these amazing excursions and grasp the interconnectedness of the Icy environment.

The Cold Owl and Environmental Change

The Icy is changing at an extraordinary speed because of environmental change. Warming temperatures, contracting ocean ice, and changed movement designs are influencing the whole Icy biological system, including the Icy owl. As the tundra warms, the owl's living space and prey are moving, introducing new difficulties to its endurance.

This section investigates the effect of environmental change on the Cold owl and its shaky situation in a quickly impacting world. It additionally talks about protection endeavors pointed toward saving this notable species.

The Icy Owl's Sonata in Craftsmanship and Writing

The Cold owl has made a permanent imprint on workmanship and writing. Its distinct excellence and ethereal presence have enlivened specialists, journalists, and writers for quite a long time. This part digs into the masterpieces and writing that give proper respect to the Cold owl, displaying how it has caught the human creative mind.

From canvases to sonnets, the Cold owl's sonata reverberations through the domains of human imagination, a demonstration of its getting through charm.

A Call to Safeguard the Cold

In the last part, we complete the cycle, perceiving the significance of protecting the Cold and its notorious animals, like the Icy owl. The part features the basic requirement for preservation endeavors and global collaboration to safeguard this delicate and indispensable environment.

As the Cold changes, the frightful call of the Icy owl fills in as an impactful sign of the deplorable act expected to defend this special district and its exceptional occupants.

8.1 Introduction to Arctic Owls

The Cold, an immense and distant locale portrayed by its unforgiving environment and shocking scenes, is home to an assortment of exceptional and striking natural life. Among the many interesting animals that call the Icy home, the Cold owls stand apart as quite possibly of the most famous and perplexing specie. These magnificent flying predators have adjusted to the outrageous states of the Cold, exhibiting a scope of wonderful highlights and ways of behaving that make them genuinely exceptional. In this extensive prologue to Cold owls, we will investigate their actual qualities, natural surroundings, hunting methodologies, and the job they play in the Icy biological system.

1. **Scientific categorization and Order**

   Cold owls have a place with the family Strigidae, which incorporates an extensive variety of owl species viewed as around the world. Inside this family, the Cold owl is grouped under the variety Bubo, and its logical name is Bubo scandiacus. The Bubo variety incorporates a few other owl animal categories, however the Cold owl stands apart for its remarkable variations to life in the super Icy circumstances.

   The Icy owl is at times alluded to as the "Cold Owl" because of its striking all-white plumage, which fills in as fantastic disguise against the snow-shrouded scenes of the Icy.

This disguise is especially significant for these owls, as they basically chase during the day and need to mix in with their environmental factors to stay away from identification by their prey.

2. **Actual Attributes**

Plumage: The most distinctive element of Icy owls is their unmistakable all-white plumage, which separates them from most other owl species. This white plumage assists them with mixing in with their frigid climate and furnishes them with successful disguise while hunting. In any case, it's important that not all Cold owls are totally white; a few people might have more obscure markings on their quills.

Size: Cold owls are somewhat huge birds, with a typical wingspan of around 150 cm (5 feet) and a body length of 55-70 cm (22-28 inches). Guys are regularly more modest than females, and their size permits them to catch an extensive variety of prey.

Bill and Claws: Like different raptors, Cold owls have solid noses and sharp claws intended for getting a handle on and catching prey. Their claws are especially appropriate for getting and clutching little well evolved creatures and birds, which make up a huge part of their eating regimen.

Facial Circle: Icy owls have a facial plate, a round plan of plumes around their eyes that coordinates sound towards their ears. This transformation permits them to find prey by sound, a urgent expertise for hunting in the Icy's boundless expanses where perceivability can be restricted.

3. **Environment**

The Icy is an immense and testing climate, portrayed by outrageous chilly, solid breezes, and long, brutal winters. Cold owls have advanced to flourish in this difficult climate, and their environment ranges across the Icy tundra and subarctic districts of North America, Eurasia, and, surprisingly, a few pieces of northern Canada. A portion of the critical elements of their living space include:

Tundra: Icy owls are appropriate to the treeless tundra scene, which comprises of immense regions of open landscape with insignificant vegetation. This climate furnishes them with clear views for hunting and an overflow of little warm blooded creatures, their essential prey.

Settling Locales: Cold owls frequently home on the ground, making homes in shallow dejections or on rough outcrops. They may likewise utilize deserted homes of different birds, like ptarmigans, for their own reproducing.

Occasional Relocation: Icy owls are traveling birds, and their developments are intently attached to the accessibility of prey. During years when their essential prey, like lemmings, is scant, Cold owls might move south looking for food. This movement is a method for surviving that assists them with adapting to the capricious food supply in the Icy.

4. **Conduct and Variations**

Nighttime and Diurnal Action: Dissimilar to numerous owl species, Cold owls are diurnal, and that implies they are dynamic during the day. This transformation is a reaction to the consistent sunlight of the Icy summer, and it permits them to make the most of the lengthy hunting potential open doors.

Hunting Technique: Cold owls principally chase little warm blooded creatures, like lemmings, voles, and ptarmigans. They utilize their sharp vision to detect prey from a good ways and afterward dip down with accuracy to catch it. Their quiet flight, a trait of numerous owl species, empowers them to move toward prey without cautioning it.

Regional Way of behaving: Icy owls are regional birds and are known to shield their settling and hunting domains from different owls. They might take part in airborne showcases and vocalizations to attest predominance and safeguard their assets.

Life span: Cold owls can have generally lengthy life expectancies, for certain people satisfying 10 years in nature. Their endurance relies upon tracking down adequate food and effectively replicating in the difficult Cold circumstances.

Rearing and Multiplication: Cold owls ordinarily breed in the spring and late-spring when food is more plentiful. Guys take part in romance shows, and coordinates might frame enduring bonds. The female lays a grip of eggs in a ground home, and the two guardians share the obligations of brooding and taking care of the youthful owlets.

Cover: The all-white plumage of Icy owls gives them viable disguise against the snow, making it hard for likely hunters and prey to detect them. This cover is significant for their endurance in the Icy's open territory.

5. **Job in the Icy Biological system**

Icy owls assume a critical part in the Icy environment as both top hunters and supporters of biological system balance.

Hunter Prey Connections: Cold owls are top hunters in their environment, going after little vertebrates and birds. Their essential prey, like lemmings and voles, can altogether affect the vegetation of the tundra. By controlling the number of inhabitants in these herbivores, Cold owls in a roundabout way impact the plant networks in the district.

Biological system Administrations: Icy owls assist with keeping up with the equilibrium of the environment by controlling the populaces of their prey species. This, thus, upholds other untamed life and the general wellbeing of the Icy environment.

Marker Species: The presence and wealth of Cold owls can act as signs of the wellbeing and soundness of Icy biological systems. Changes in their populaces might flag more extensive ecological changes, remembering shifts for prey populaces and natural surroundings quality.

6. **Protection Status**

While Icy owls are not at present recorded as compromised or imperiled, their populaces can be impacted by different ecological variables. Environmental change and territory aggravation can affect their settling and hunting grounds, while vacillations in prey populaces can influence their endurance.

Preservation endeavors in the Icy frequently center around saving the honesty of the tundra territory and safeguarding the different species that rely upon it, including Cold owls. Observing and research drives are fundamental to grasp the status and patterns of their populaces, guaranteeing their drawn out endurance.

8.2 The Enchanting Hoots of Arctic Owls

The Icy, a locale of outrageous chilly, immense fields, and staggering normal magnificence, is home to a heap of entrancing untamed life species, each interestingly adjusted to its requesting climate. Among these momentous animals, Cold owls stand apart for their puzzling appeal and enrapturing hoots. These lofty flying predators have for some time been the subject of interest and deference, for their striking actual elements as well as for their eerie calls that reverberation through the freezing Cold scenes. In this investigation of the charming hoots of Cold owls, we will dig into their vocalizations, their importance in their territory, and the job these calls play in their endurance and rearing procedures.

1. **The Vocal Universe of Icy Owls**

   Icy owls, logically known as Bubo scandiacus, have a scope of vocalizations that are essentially as unmistakable as their appearance. While not generally so various as certain larks or parrots, the vocalizations of Icy owls fill fundamental needs in their lives, from correspondence to route and romance.

   Hooting: The hoot is maybe the most famous sound related with owls, and Cold owls are no exemption. Their hooting is a profound, thunderous sound that extends significant distances in the Cold's open landscape. The hoot is frequently utilized for regional stamping and keeping separation between adjoining owl matches.

Shrieking: Cold owls can create shrieking calls, particularly during experiences with possible dangers or in light of seen gatecrashers in their domain. These calls are piercing and sharp, filling in as an advance notice sign to likely foes.

Clacking: During romance and the raising of youthful owlets, Cold owls might utilize milder cackling sounds to convey. These clacks are regularly gentler and less obvious than their regional hooting, making a more private correspondence channel inside the pair.

2. **The Job of Vocalizations in Icy Owl Conduct**

Icy owls are single birds for a significant part of the year, and their vocalizations assume a critical part in laying out and keeping up with an area, drawing in mates, and safeguarding their young. How about we investigate how these vocalizations impact their way of behaving and collaborations with the climate.

Regional Guard: The hooting calls of Icy owls act as regional markers, permitting people to guarantee and safeguard a particular region of the tundra. These domains are fundamental for getting hunting grounds and rearing locales. While a meddling owl enters a region, hooting duels between the occupant and the gatecrasher might follow, frequently prompting one of the owls withdrawing to keep up with harmony.

Romance and Mating: During the reproducing season, Cold owls depend on vocalizations to draw in possible mates. The male's hooting calls are a significant piece of romance presentations, and an effective song can win the blessing of a female. When a couple has reinforced, milder cackling sounds might be traded as a feature of their romance customs.

Raising Youthful: After effectively drawing in a mate and reproducing, Cold owls keep on involving vocalizations in their parental jobs. The gentler, more private cackling sounds are utilized for speaking with their young owlets. These calls assist the guardians with planning food conveyances, share liabilities, and keep up with the family bond.

3. **Methods for surviving and Vocal Mimicry**

   The Icy climate can challenge, with food accessibility differing from one year to another. Cold owls display noteworthy step by step processes for surviving, and their vocal mimicry is one such transformation.

   Disguise and Quiet: Cold owls are prestigious for their secretive white plumage, which assists them with mixing into the frigid scene and stay stowed away from prey and hunters. Be that as it may, their vocalizations are one more part of their step by step process for surviving. While hunting, they fly quietly, utilizing specific wing plumes to diminish clamor and guarantee secrecy while moving toward their prey.

   Vocal Mimicry: Icy owls are known for imitating the calls of different birds, especially during the reproducing season. This mimicry fills numerous needs. By mimicking different birds, they can draw in more modest prey creatures, similar to birds, which might move toward in light of the clear pain calls. Along these lines, Cold owls extend their menu choices, guaranteeing they can find food in any event, during lean years when their essential prey, like lemmings, is scant.

4. **The Job of Vocalizations in Rearing Achievement**

   Cold owls regularly breed in the spring and late-spring, which presents one of a kind difficulties in the Icy climate.

Their vocalizations assume an imperative part in guaranteeing reproducing achievement and the endurance of their young.

Monogamous Bonds: Icy owls are known for framing monogamous matches, and their vocalizations are vital to keeping up with these bonds. Fruitful romance and the trading of vocalizations reinforce the pair's obligation to each other, guaranteeing that they collaborate in the raising of their young.

Coordination of Parental Obligations: When a couple of Icy owls has effectively reproduced and has youthful owlets to really focus on, their vocalizations assist with planning the division of work between guardians. Cackling sounds are milder and less obvious, permitting guardians to impart without making potential hunters aware of the area of their home.

Safeguarding the Home: Icy owls are industrious guardians and effectively protect their homes and youthful against possible dangers, like ruthless birds. When confronted with risk, they might create shrieking calls to deflect the gatecrashers and safeguard their posterity.

5. **Preservation Suggestions**

While Cold owls are not right now named imperiled, they truly do confront different protection challenges. These difficulties are frequently intently attached to the evolving environment, which can influence the accessibility of their essential prey, like lemmings, and their favored settling and hunting living spaces.

Preservation endeavors in the Icy spotlight on safeguarding the respectability of the tundra biological system, which Cold owls depend on. Checking their populaces and concentrating on their vocalizations can give significant bits of knowledge into the soundness of the Icy climate and likely effects from environmental change and human exercises.

6. **The Charming Allure of Icy Owl Hoots**

Cold owls, with their charming hoots and enamoring calls, have a novel spot in the regular world. Their vocalizations, profoundly interlaced with their way of behaving and methods for surviving, add an additional layer of interest to these noteworthy birds.

For quite a long time, the frightful hoots of Icy owls have roused legends, stories, and social importance in the districts they possess. They are an image of the secretive and stunning Cold wild, a symbol of the lofty and untamed scene they call home.

8.3 The Survival Strategies of Arctic Owls

1. **Prologue to Icy Owls**
   Icy owls are a types of owl remarkably adjusted to the super cold and testing states of the Icy. They have a place with the family Strigidae, and their logical name, Bubo scandiacus, stresses their characterization under the Bubo class. Among the most striking elements that put them aside is their all-white plumage, which fills in as compelling cover in the frigid scenes of the Cold.

2. **Actual Transformations**
   Icy owls have developed a scope of actual variations that permit them to flourish in their threatening climate. These variations assist them with adapting to the super chilly, furious breezes, and long, dim winters of the Icy.
   Protection: Icy owls have thick, layered plumage that gives excellent protection against the virus. Their plumes trap a layer of air near their bodies, making a successful boundary against heat misfortune. Moreover, their plumage is waterproof, keeping dampness from entering and influencing

their protecting properties.

Disguise: Their notorious all-white plumage permits Icy owls to mix flawlessly into the snow-shrouded scene, offering successful covering from both prey and hunters. This disguise assists them with hunting undetected and decreases the possibilities becoming prey themselves.

Padded Feet: Dissimilar to some other owl species, Cold owls have feathers on their legs and feet. These padded extremities give extra protection and security against the bone chilling temperatures of the tundra.

Round Facial Circle: Icy owls, in the same way as other different owls, have a roundabout facial plate of plumes that assists channel with sounding to their ears. This element empowers them to find prey by sound, an important expertise in the huge and open Cold scene.

3. **Hunting Procedures**

Icy owls are diurnal trackers, essentially dynamic during the day. Their hunting procedures are finely tuned to the difficulties of the Icy tundra and the way of behaving of their prey.

Quiet Flight: Like most owls, Icy owls have developed a particular wing structure that considers essentially quiet flight. This variation is essential for secretive hunting, empowering them to move toward their prey without making clamor that could alarm their quarry.

Sharp Visual perception: Icy owls have superb vision, which they use to detect prey from a good ways. Their sharp vision is appropriate to the open tundra, where they can see potential prey like lemmings, voles, and ptarmigans from far off.

Regional Way of behaving: Icy owls are regional birds and effectively guard their hunting grounds. They might participate in aeronautical showcases and vocalizations to state strength and shield their region from gatecrashers.

4. **Conduct Transformations**

The methods for surviving of Icy owls reach out past their actual transformations and hunting strategies. Their ways of behaving are likewise finely tuned to adapt to the difficulties of the Cold climate.

Nighttime and Diurnal Movement: Icy owls are diurnal trackers, adjusted to the persistent sunlight of the Cold summer. This transformation permits them to make the most of the lengthy hunting open doors during the short Cold summer.

Occasional Relocation: Icy owls are itinerant birds, and their developments are intently attached to the accessibility of prey. During years when their essential prey, like lemmings, is scant, Cold owls might relocate south looking for food. This relocation is a method for surviving that assists them with adapting to the flighty food supply in the Icy.

Regional Guard: Icy owls are known for their regional way of behaving, protecting their settling and hunting domains from different owls. This territoriality guarantees they approach the assets required for endurance.

5. **Rearing and Generation**

The rearing and regenerative ways of behaving of Icy owls are one more part of their method for surviving, empowering them to keep up with their populace in the difficult Cold climate.

Timing: Icy owls regularly breed in the spring and late-spring, exploiting the expanded food accessibility during this period.

Monogamous Bonds: Icy owls structure monogamous matches, and their solid bonds are critical for effective generation. The pair's common collaboration in raising their young upgrades their rearing achievement.

Settling: Icy owls frequently home on the ground, making homes in shallow melancholies or on rough outcrops. They may likewise utilize deserted homes of different birds, like ptarmigans, for their own reproducing.

Hatching and Nurturing: Both male and female Icy owls share responsibilities regarding brooding the eggs and raising the youthful. This helpful nurturing guarantees the endurance and advancement of their posterity.

Vocalizations: Vocalizations assume a part in the reproducing conduct of Cold owls. Guys take part in romance shows, and coordinates might trade delicate clacking sounds as a component of their romance customs and parental correspondence.

6. **Job in the Icy Environment**

Icy owls assume a critical part in the Cold biological system as both top hunters and supporters of environment balance.

Hunter Prey Connections: Cold owls are dominant hunters in their living space, going after little well evolved creatures, birds, and even fish. Their essential prey, like lemmings and voles, can fundamentally affect the vegetation of the tundra. By controlling the number of inhabitants in these herbivores, Icy owls by implication impact the plant networks in the locale.

Biological system Administrations: Cold owls assist with keeping up with the equilibrium of the environment by controlling the populaces of their prey species. This, thus, upholds other natural life and the general soundness of the Cold biological system.

Pointer Species: The presence and overflow of Icy owls can act as signs of the wellbeing and steadiness of Cold environments. Changes in their populaces might flag more extensive ecological changes, remembering shifts for prey populaces and living space quality.

7. **Protection Status**

While Icy owls are not right now recorded as compromised or jeopardized, their populaces can be impacted by different ecological elements. Environmental change, natural surroundings aggravation, and variances in prey populaces are a portion of the difficulties they face.

Preservation endeavors in the Icy frequently center around safeguarding the trustworthiness of the tundra natural surroundings and safeguarding the different species that rely upon it, including Icy owls. Checking and research drives are fundamental for grasping the status and patterns of their populaces, guaranteeing their drawn out endurance.

8. **Difficulties and Dangers**

The methods for surviving of Icy owls are being tried by progressing ecological changes and human exercises. A portion of the difficulties and dangers they face include:

Environmental Change: Cold owls are powerless with the impacts of environmental change, which remember shifts for prey populaces and living space adjustments. Warming temperatures can upset the fragile equilibrium of the Cold environment, influencing the accessibility of their essential food sources.

Living space Aggravation: Human exercises, like asset extraction and foundation advancement, can disturb Icy owl natural surroundings and settling locales. Aggravations can prompt deserted homes, diminished reproducing achievement, and expanded weakness to predation.

Contamination: Toxins, like pesticides, can aggregate in the Icy pecking order, influencing the wellbeing of both Icy owls and their prey species. These foreign substances can debilitate Cold owl populaces, making them more helpless to ecological stressors.

Aggravation by People: The travel industry and examination exercises in the Cold can unexpectedly upset Icy owls, influencing their hunting and rearing ways of behaving. Rules and guidelines are fundamental to limit human effect on these birds.

9. Preservation Endeavors

Preservation endeavors pointed toward saving Cold owls and their natural surroundings are fundamental to guaranteeing their endurance. A few systems and drives include:

Safeguarded Regions: Laying out and keeping up with safeguarded regions in the Cold is basic for protecting the environment of Icy owls and other untamed life. These regions give safe reproducing and searching grounds.

Exploration and Observing: Logical examination is major for grasping the populace elements, conduct, and biological jobs of Icy owls. Observing projects can assist with distinguishing early indications of populace declines or natural changes.

Environmental Change Moderation: Endeavors to relieve environmental change can assist with keeping up with the soundness of Icy biological systems. Decreasing ozone depleting substance outflows and supporting preservation measures are fundamental for the drawn out endurance of Cold owls.

Instruction and Effort: Bringing issues to light about the significance of Cold owls and the delicacy of the Icy biological system is fundamental for collecting public help and upholding for their preservation.

Dependable The travel industry: The travel industry in the Cold can give financial advantages to neighborhood networks. Notwithstanding, it is indispensable to guarantee that travel industry exercises are directed dependably, with negligible effect on natural life and their territories.

Territory Reclamation: Endeavors to reestablish and safeguard basic Icy environments can help Icy owls as well as other natural life species in the locale.

8.4 An Arctic Owl-inspired Lullaby

In the immense, quiet spread of the Icy, where the gnawing cold and perpetual whiteness can appear to be immovable, there exists an animal that has long caught the creative mind of the people who set out to wander into its frozen domain. The Icy owl, otherwise called the frigid owl, is a glorious and puzzling bird that flourishes in the most extreme of conditions. With its blanketed plumage and puncturing brilliant eyes, it has turned into an image of the Icy's untamed magnificence and versatility. This superb bird has motivated innumerable stories and melodies, however today, we dive into the production of a children's song that gives proper respect to the Icy owl and the quiet wizardry it brings to the frozen evening.

Prologue to the Icy Owl

Before we leave on our melodic excursion, we should initially familiarize ourselves with the Cold owl. The cold owl, Bubo scandiacus, is an enormous, transcendently white owl species that occupies the circumpolar locales of the Northern Half of the globe. It is maybe generally popular for its particular appearance: a layer of unadulterated white quills dotted with dull, unpredictable examples that look like sensitive snowflakes, and its enormous, round, brilliant yellow eyes that convey insight beyond anything that can be described. The Icy owl is an expert of its current circumstance, impeccably adjusted to the unforgiving Cold circumstances.

This heavenly bird is an image of effortlessness, strength, and the untamed magnificence of the Cold wild. It gets through the freezing temperatures and outrageous separation of the polar areas, where not many different animals try to wander. The frigid owl has for some time been a subject of interest, motivating specialists, scholars, and performers the same to commend its ethereal presence in the frosty tundra.

The Tune of the Cold Evening

To make a children's song enlivened by the Cold owl, we should initially drench ourselves in the pith of this magnificent animal and the tranquil world it occupies. In the Icy, the evenings are long and calm, with a significant quietness that wraps the scene.

The breeze murmurs mysteries across the frozen territories, and Aurora Borealis dance overhead, projecting a supernatural shine over the frigid fields. It is inside this quiet domain that our bedtime song comes to fruition.

The cradlesong starts with a delicate, fragile song played on a piano, copying the sensitive impressions of the Icy owl as it nimbly travels through the snow. The notes are slow and think, repeating the bird's sluggish speed. As the song unfurls, it continuously presents a woodwind, representing the breeze that breadths across the Icy scene. The flute's delicate, breezy tones make a feeling of serenity and quiet, similar as the tranquil evenings of the Cold.

The Quiet Flight

One of the most exceptional attributes of the Cold owl is its quiet flight. The quills of these owls are extraordinarily adjusted to limit clamor, permitting them to chase their prey with covertness and accuracy. This component turns into a focal component in our children's song, addressing the owl's effortless way to deal with life.

As the cradlesong proceeds, the piano and woodwind songs mix flawlessly with the presentation of a string segment. The strings summon the Cold owl's quiet flight, with their delicate, legato notes that copy the easy coasting of the bird through the chilly air. The music steadily works in power, catching the bird's assurance and concentration as it chases after its prey in the Cold obscurity.

The Brilliant Eyes

The Cold owl's brilliant yellow eyes are quite possibly of its most striking element. These eyes are not only a demonstration of the bird's actual excellence yet in addition an impression of its knowledge and mindfulness. Our cradlesong honors these dazzling eyes through a change in the creation.

As the cradlesong advances, the piano and woodwind take on a more melodic, expressive job, mirroring the owl's significant association with it's general surroundings. The strings keep on giving the setting, making a feeling of serenity, while the piano and woodwind inspire the owl's curious look. The music takes on a hotter tone, representing the insight and profundity concealed inside the Icy owl's eyes.

The Dance of Aurora Borealis

The Icy is known for its stunning presentations of Aurora Borealis, a characteristic peculiarity that captivates all who witness it. The dynamic tones and effortless development of the auroras rouse the following period of our children's song.

The coordination grows to incorporate a full ensemble, including violins, cellos, and metal instruments.

These components address the loftiness of Aurora Borealis and the endlessness of the Cold scene. The tune takes on an additional dynamic and clearing quality, much the same as the twirling, bright dance of the auroras in the night sky.

The Cradlesong's Crescendo

As our cradlesong arrives at its crescendo, it mirrors the zenith of the Icy owl's excursion through the frozen evening. The piano, woodwind, strings, and full ensemble converge into an amicable and genuinely charged organization that embodies the loftiness of the Icy scene, the insight of the owl's brilliant eyes, and the quietness of its quiet flight.

The Goal

With the peak of the cradlesong, the music progressively progresses, representing the Icy owl's re-visitation of its singular roost in the frozen wild. The piano and woodwind return to their underlying, fragile tune, and the symphonic components gradually disappear. The last notes bring a feeling of conclusion, reflecting the owl's re-visitation of its home, content and settled.

The Cradlesong's Message

Our Icy owl-roused bedtime song embodies the substance of the cold owl and the Icy scene. It honors the owl's effortlessness, versatility, and astuteness, while additionally praising the serenity of the Icy evening. In the quiet of this frozen world, where the Cold owl rules as an image of magnificence and versatility, we find motivation for a cradlesong that relieves the spirit and summons the sorcery of the far North.

Chapter 9

The Narwhal's Whistle

1.1. The Narwhal: A Wonder of the Icy

In the remote and cold waters of the Icy, there exists an animal that has caught the human creative mind for quite a long time. The narwhal, logically known as Monodon monoceros, is frequently alluded to as the "unicorn of the ocean" because of its particular long, spiraled ivory tusk jutting from its upper jaw. Be that as it may, past this notorious tusk, the narwhal holds another secret — the mysterious narwhal's whistle.

1.2. The Secret of the Narwhal's Whistle

The narwhal's whistle is a one of a kind vocalization created by these subtle marine vertebrates. It isn't only a sound; it addresses a mystery — a complicated riddle of science, physical science, culture, and persona. These whistles have been a wellspring of interest, motivation, and logical request, filling in as a significant association among people and one of the Cold's most subtle occupants.

1.3. Reason and Extension

This top to bottom investigation tries to unwind the narwhal's reality, zeroing in basically on its unbelievable tusk, its confusing whistle, and the multifaceted transaction between these components. Through this 4000-word venture, we expect to reveal insight into the narwhal's whistle and its importance with regards to the more extensive Icy biological system and human interest.

The Narwhal: Unicorn of the Ocean

2.1. Life systems and Physiology

To comprehend the narwhal's whistle, it is crucial for first handle the interesting life systems and physiology of these amazing animals. Narwhals are medium-sized marine warm blooded creatures that can arrive at lengths of up to 16 feet. Their most particular element is, obviously, their long, twisting tusk, which can develop to be a few feet long. This tusk is really an extended tooth, which guys foster all through their lives.

2.2. Developmental History

The narwhal's developmental history is a captivating story that associates them to other marine warm blooded creatures, including belugas and orcas. Understanding their developmental starting points can give important bits of knowledge into their particular variations and ways of behaving.

2.3. Social Importance

Narwhals have been socially influential for native Cold people group for a really long time. Their tusks have been utilized as a wellspring of ivory, a material that has been created into different instruments and fine art. Investigating the social meaning of narwhals and their tusks offers a brief look into the well established associations between these animals and the native people groups of the Icy.

2.4. Narwhals in the Cold Environment

Narwhals are not secluded animals; they are basic to the Icy biological system. This segment investigates their job in the pecking order, their associations with different species, and the more extensive biological effect of their presence.

The Baffling Whistle

3.1. Authentic Records

The narwhal's whistle has been referenced in authentic records going back hundreds of years. From the earliest experiences of European pioneers with these perplexing animals to native Inuit stories, there is a rich embroidery of verifiable records that allude to the narwhal's vocalizations.

3.2. Logical Investigations

The logical investigation of the narwhal's whistle started vigorously in the twentieth hundred years. Analysts have utilized different procedures, including hydroacoustics, to record and examine these vocalizations. We will dig into the early examinations that gave the establishment to our ongoing comprehension of the narwhal's whistle.

3.3. Legends and Fantasies

Over the entire course of time, the narwhal has been the subject of various legends and fables. These accounts frequently trait supernatural or enchanted properties to the narwhal and its tusk. Understanding the fantasies and legends encompassing these animals adds a layer of interest to the secret of their whistles.

3.4. Current Investigation

Lately, progresses in innovation and research strategies have considered greater investigation of the narwhal's vocalizations. This segment will feature current logical endeavors and their commitments to how we might interpret the narwhal's whistle.

Narwhals and Their Whistles: A Profound Jump

4.1. Correspondence in the Icy

The Icy is a tremendous, remote, and testing climate. How do narwhals utilize their whistles to speak with one another in these frigid waters? This segment investigates the significance of vocalizations in the narwhal's social and environmental setting.

4.2. Whistle Attributes

What do narwhal whistles really sound like? This segment gives a point by point examination of the acoustic properties of these vocalizations, including pitch, recurrence, and span.

4.3. Whistle Creation Components

How do narwhals create these novel sounds? We will look at the physiological instruments behind narwhal whistle creation and the job of their particular life systems.

4.4. Hypotheses on Whistle Capabilities

Scientists have proposed different hypotheses with respect to the elements of narwhal whistles. This segment will investigate these hypotheses, including correspondence, route, and possible natural jobs.

The Cold Domain: Narwhals' Environment

5.1. Icy Sea: A Chilly, Brutal Climate

The Icy Sea is a distinct and unforgiving climate, making it a difficult territory for narwhals. Understanding the attributes of this district is critical to valuing the circumstances under which these animals flourish.

5.2. Narwhal Movement Examples

Narwhals are known for their significant distance movements. This segment will dive into the transient examples of narwhals, revealing insight into the broad excursions they embrace every year.

5.3. Taking care of and Generation

What do narwhals eat, and how would they recreate? This part investigates their dietary inclinations and regenerative methodologies, featuring the basic job of the narwhal's current circumstance.

Narwhals and Human Collaboration

6.1. Conventional Inuit Hunting

For quite a long time, native Inuit people group have depended on narwhals as a wellspring of food and materials. We will look at the customary hunting rehearses and the social meaning of narwhals in Inuit social orders.

6.2. Preservation Endeavors

As narwhals face new difficulties, protection endeavors have acquired significance. This part will talk about the drives pointed toward safeguarding these animals and their delicate living space.

6.3. Environmental Change and Its Effect

Environmental change represents a huge danger to the Icy and its occupants. We will investigate the particular effects of environmental change on narwhals and their current circumstance.

The Narwhal's Whistle in Craftsmanship and Culture

7.1. Native Workmanship and Stories

Native Icy societies have a profound association with narwhals, which is reflected in their craft, stories, and customs. We will dive into the imaginative and social portrayals of narwhals in these networks.

7.2. Narwhals in Writing and Craftsmanship

Narwhals have additionally transformed the more extensive universe of writing and workmanship. This segment will investigate their presence in books, canvases, and different types of imaginative articulation.

7.3. The Whistle's Effect on Music

The narwhal's whistle has even tracked down its direction into music. We will find how the strange call of the narwhal has roused artists and arrangers from the beginning of time.

Whistle Exploration: Logical Disclosures

8.1. Hydroacoustic Studies

Hydroacoustics is a vital device in concentrating on the narwhal's whistle. This part will make sense of the techniques used to record and dissect these vocalizations underneath the Cold waves.

8.2. Narwhal Vocalizations

What have researchers found about the narwhal's vocal collection? This part will give experiences into the range of sounds narwhals produce past their unique whistles.

8.3. Whistle Planning and Investigation

Planning the circulation of narwhal whistles and dissecting their acoustic elements has given important information. We will investigate the discoveries of these examinations and their suggestions.

The Mission for Figuring out: Current Exploration

9.1. Challenges in Narwhal Perception

Concentrating on narwhals right at home is no simple assignment. This part will detail the difficulties scientists face while attempting to notice and record these tricky animals.

9.2. Ebb and flow Exploration Drives

What are the most recent examination drives zeroed in on narwhals and their whistles? We will feature progressing projects and their expected commitments to our comprehension.

9.3. Innovative Progressions

Propels in innovation have enormously upgraded our capacity to concentrate on narwhals. We will examine the apparatuses and developments that have reformed narwhal research.

The Moral Aspect: Preservation and Government assistance

10.1. Safeguarding Narwhals and Their Current circumstance

Protection endeavors are critical to the conservation of narwhals and their Cold environment. We will investigate the moral and natural components of these endeavors.

10.2. Adjusting Science and Preservation

Protection should be offset with the requirement for logical exploration. This part will address the fragile harmony between safeguarding narwhals and propelling our insight.

10.3. Future Possibilities

What does the future hold for narwhals and their whistles? We will conjecture on the difficulties and open doors that lie ahead for these one of a kind animals.

The Narwhal's Whistle and Human Interest

11.1. The Charm of the Puzzling

What is it about the narwhal's whistle that keeps on enthralling human interest? This segment will investigate the getting through allure of the mysterious call of the unicorn of the ocean.

11.2. Our Association with Nature

The narwhal's whistle fills in as a sign of our interconnectedness with the normal world. We will examine the more extensive ramifications of this association for our relationship with the climate.

11.3. The Whistle as an Image of Marvel

In a world loaded up with secrets, the narwhal's whistle represents the marvel and enchantment of the regular world. This segment will dig into the meaning of the narwhal's whistle as an image of wonder and motivation.

9.1 Introduction to the Narwhal

The narwhal, Monodon monoceros, frequently alluded to as the "unicorn of the ocean," is an interesting and baffling marine well evolved creature that possesses the freezing waters of the Icy. This amazing animal has spellbound human creative mind and logical interest for quite a long time, because of its unmistakable long, twisting tusk and its strange submerged vocalizations. In this presentation, we will leave on an excursion to find the universe of the narwhal, investigating its science, transformative history, social importance, and biological job inside the Cold environment.

1. **Life structures and Physiology of the Narwhal**

    Narwhals are medium-sized marine warm blooded creatures, with guys regularly arriving at lengths of up to 16 feet, while females are marginally more modest. In any case, their most striking component, and the one for which they are most popular, is the long, twisting tusk that juts from their upper jaw. This tusk, which is really a changed tooth, can reach out to lengths of a few feet, making it perhaps of the most notable and baffling component in the set of all animals.

    The motivation behind the narwhal's tusk has been the subject of much hypothesis and logical examination. A few speculations propose that it could act as a tactile organ, assisting narwhals with exploring their frosty climate or find prey. Others suggest that it assumes a part in friendly collaborations or mate determination. Regardless of broad exploration, the full capability of the tusk stays a subject of progressing study and discussion.

2. Transformative History of the Narwhal

To comprehend the narwhal's remarkable elements, investigating its transformative history is fundamental. Narwhals have a place with the Monodontidae family, which incorporates another Icy occupant, the beluga whale (Delphinapterus leucas). Hereditary and morphological investigations propose that narwhals share a typical progenitor with belugas, and their developmental ways have separated to adjust to various natural specialties.

The narwhal's particular tusk is a momentous illustration of transformation because of the difficulties of its current circumstance. The tusks develop all through a male narwhal's life, with every year's development framing another twisting layer. This powerful development is a demonstration of the surprising transformative variations that have permitted narwhals to flourish in the brutal Icy oceans.

3. Social Meaning of the Narwhal

Narwhals have held social importance for native Cold people group for quite a long time. Inuit people groups, who have lived in the Cold for ages, have depended on narwhals as a wellspring of food and materials. The narwhal's ivory tusk, specifically, has been profoundly valued for its solidness and usefulness, and making different instruments and imaginative expressions has been utilized.

The social meaning of narwhals stretches out past their down to earth utility. Inuit folklore and legends include narwhals conspicuously, frequently ascribing profound or otherworldly characteristics to these animals. The narwhal's tusk, accepted to be the horn of an ocean soul, plays had a focal impact in native stories and customs, associating these networks with the normal world and their firmly established regard for the Cold climate.

4. Narwhals in the Cold Biological system

Narwhals are not confined animals; they are fundamental parts of the Icy biological system. Their eating routine essentially comprises of fish and squid, making them a critical connection in the Cold marine pecking order. In this cruel climate, they are both hunter and prey, adding to the equilibrium of this delicate environment.

Their job as both hunter and prey has gradually expanding influences on the Icy biological system. The hunters that depend on narwhals for food incorporate orcas and polar bears, while their prey things might be affected by narwhal predation. Understanding the elements of these connections is significant for grasping the more extensive natural setting in which narwhals exist.

As we dive further into the universe of narwhals, we will unwind the secrets encompassing their novel vocalizations, the supposed "narwhal's whistle." These submerged sounds have charmed researchers, voyagers, and native people groups for a really long time, and they offer a window into the many-sided and interconnected trap of life in the Icy oceans.

9.2 The Mystical Whistles of Narwhals

1. **Outline of Narwhals**

   Narwhals, frequently alluded to as the "unicorns of the ocean," are slippery marine warm blooded creatures that occupy the bone chilling waters of the Cold. These cryptic animals are known for their long, winding tusks, which can arrive at lengths of up to ten feet, and their interesting vocalizations, frequently portrayed as whistles. Notwithstanding their relationship with fantasies and legends, narwhals are genuine, living animals that have intrigued researchers, adventurers, and societies for quite a long time.

2. **The Whistles of Narwhals**

   Among the numerous amazing attributes of narwhals, their capacity to create strange and tormenting whistles sticks out. These whistles are a fundamental piece of their correspondence and social connections, however they likewise hold a specific mysterious charm. The motivation behind this extensive investigation is to dive into the universe of narwhal whistles, uncover their insider facts, and figure out their social and logical importance.

3. Otherworldly and Social Importance

Since the beginning of time, narwhals and their whistles have been adored and mythologized by different societies all over the planet. From stories of unicorns to Inuit legends, narwhals play had a noticeable impact in the aggregate creative mind. This work will analyze the mysterious and social meaning of narwhals and their whistles, as well as their place in contemporary society.

The Unicorn of the Ocean

1. **Actual Qualities**
   Narwhals have particular actual elements, including their long tusks, smoothed out bodies, and a mottled grayish-blue hue. These transformations are fundamental for their endurance in the unforgiving Cold climate, where they spend quite a bit of their lives.

2. **Environment and Dispersion**
   Narwhals are basically tracked down in the Icy Sea and nearby oceans, where they explore the frigid waters and look for shelter in open leads. Their transitory examples and occasional ways of behaving will be investigated, revealing insight into their perplexing connection with the changing polar climate.

3. **Taking care of and Conduct**

Narwhals are meat eating animals, principally benefiting from fish and squid. Their hunting procedures and social conduct will be analyzed, giving understanding into the difficulties they face as they continued looking for food.

The Whistle Peculiarity

1. **Disclosure of Narwhal Whistles**

   The presence of narwhal whistles became known to established researchers somewhat as of late, and the disclosure was met with interest and interest. We will investigate the early experiences and the spearheading endeavors to study and record these submerged vocalizations.

2. **Special Sound Creation**

   Understanding how narwhals produce their whistles is vital to interpreting their vocalizations. The life systems and mechanics behind narwhal sound creation will be revealed, revealing insight into the wellspring of these otherworldly whistles.

3. **Open Capabilities**

Narwhals utilize their whistles for different purposes, including route, social association, and perhaps mate fascination. We will dig into the complexities of narwhal correspondence and how whistles assume a vital part in their regular routines.

IV. Narwhals in Science and Preservation

1. **Concentrating on Narwhals through Sound**

   The investigation of narwhal whistles has opened up new roads for logical exploration. We will investigate the inventive techniques and advancements used to concentrate on these mysterious animals, revealing insight into their way of behaving, transitory examples, and populace elements.

2. **Narwhals and Environmental Change**

   Environmental change is significantly affecting the Cold climate, which straightforwardly influences narwhals. The ramifications of these progressions on narwhal populaces and their whistles will be inspected, alongside potential preservation endeavors.

3. **Dangers to Narwhal Populaces**

Narwhals face various dangers, including delivering traffic, hunting, and natural surroundings debasement. The effect of these dangers on narwhal populaces and the job of global protection endeavors will be talked about.

V. Supernatural and Social Importance

1. **Narwhals in Folklore**

   Narwhals have been a fundamental piece of folklore and fables in different societies, frequently connected to accounts of unicorns and other legendary animals. We will investigate these accounts and their importance in forming human view of the narwhal.

2. **Social Portrayals**

   Narwhals play had an unmistakable impact in the social practices of native Icy people group, especially the Inuit. Their craft, stories, and profound importance will be inspected, featuring the profound social associations among people and narwhals.

3. **Whistles and Their Association with Enchantment**

The secretive and tormenting narwhal whistles have a one of a kind spot in the domain of magic. We will investigate the profound and otherworldly understandings of these sounds and their effect on different conviction frameworks.

VI. The Confounding Narwhal Whistle

1. **Kinds of Narwhal Whistles**

   Narwhal whistles come in different structures, and analysts have distinguished unmistakable sorts with explicit qualities. We will investigate the different whistle types and their potential capabilities.

2. **Whistle Attributes**

   Nitty gritty investigation of narwhal whistles uncovers fascinating acoustic properties. We will dive into the complexities of these qualities, including pitch, recurrence, and term, and how they add to their persona.

3. Hypotheses and Theories

The reason for narwhal whistles stays a subject of hypothesis. Researchers have proposed a few hypotheses in regards to their job in narwhal society, and we will look at these speculations top to bottom.

VII. The Whistles' Part in Narwhal Society

1. Social Construction and Correspondence
Narwhals are known for their very close gatherings and complex correspondence. We will investigate how whistles work with social bonds, bunch union, and data trade inside narwhal cases.

2. Whistles and Proliferation
Narwhal whistles might assume a basic part in mate fascination and proliferation. We will dig into the special romance ways of behaving and the expected meaning of whistles in narwhal mating ceremonies.

3. Whistle Utilization in Day to day existence

Past mating and social cooperations, narwhal whistles probably serve different capabilities in their regular routines. We will investigate how whistles are utilized in route, scavenging, and different parts of narwhal presence.

VIII. The Human Association

1. Exploration and Protection Endeavors
Human interest and logical interest have prompted exploration and preservation drives pointed toward understanding and safeguarding narwhals and their whistles. We will investigate the spearheading exploration and preservation projects that have been instrumental in protecting these animals.

2. **Human Interest with Narwhals**
   Narwhals have caught the human creative mind for quite a long time, moving craftsmanship, writing, and mainstream society. We will dive into the different ways narwhals have impacted human innovativeness and the persevering through interest they hold.
3. **The Morals of Connecting with Narwhals**

As narwhal populaces face various dangers, the moral contemplations encompassing human connections with these animals come into sharp concentration. We will examine the moral situations encompassing narwhal hunting, the travel industry, and logical examination.

IX. The Eventual fate of Narwhals and Their Whistles

1. **Preservation Difficulties**
   The protection of narwhals and their whistles is a squeezing concern. We will analyze the continuous difficulties and possible arrangements, including peaceful accords, territory assurance, and environmental change moderation.
2. **Promising Exploration Bearings**
   The investigation of narwhals and their whistles keeps on developing. We will investigate arising research regions, like high level acoustic observing strategies, and their capability to open more secrets about these captivating animals.
3. **Rousing Activity**

Narwhals and their enchanted whistles act as a convincing image of the delicate Icy biological system. We will talk about how their story can move activity to safeguard the Icy and its novel occupants.

9.3 The Fascinating Tusk of Narwhals

The narwhal, a slippery and puzzling animal known as the "unicorn of the ocean," is portrayed by its wonderful tusk. This long, twisting tooth, which can arrive at lengths of up to ten feet, has caught the minds of individuals from the beginning of time. In this investigation, we dig into the tusk of narwhals, revealing insight into its construction, reason, and the social importance it holds.

1. **Life structures and Attributes of the Narwhal Tusk**
1. **Tusk Design**
   The narwhal's tusk is a lengthened tooth that twistings clockwise, projecting from the upper jaw of the male narwhal. This segment will dive into the underlying piece of the tusk, talking about its layers, polish, dentin, and remarkable twisting shape.
2. **Size and Development**
   Narwhal tusks shift in size, for certain people having more diminutive tusks while others have amazingly lengthy ones. We will investigate the variables affecting tusk size, development designs, and the meaning of this variety.
3. **Hue and Patina**

The hue and patina of narwhal tusks go through changes after some time. This segment will analyze the advancement of the tusk's particular patina and the elements adding to its lovely exhibit of varieties.

II. The Secrets of the Narwhal Tusk

1. **Tusk Reason and Capability**
   While the tusk of the narwhal has long fascinated researchers and lovers, its careful reason stays a subject of discussion. We will investigate the main speculations with respect to the tusk's capability, remembering its job for route, tangible discernment, and mate fascination.
2. **Tusk Tactile Capacities**
   Ongoing examination has proposed that the narwhal tusk might have tactile capabilities, with sensitive spots reaching out into the tooth. This segment will dive into the arising comprehension of the tusk as a tactile organ and the ramifications of this disclosure.
3. **Tusk Use in Day to day existence**

Perceptions of narwhal conduct propose that the tusk assumes a huge part in their day to day exercises, including hunting, correspondence, and social connections. We will analyze the different manners by which narwhals utilize their tusks in their Icy climate.

III. Social Meaning of the Narwhal Tusk

1. **Verifiable and Social Portrayals**
   Narwhal tusks have highlighted in fantasies, legends, and social customs since forever ago. We will investigate their importance in native Icy societies, as well as their depiction in writing, craftsmanship, and old stories.

2. **The Exchange and Business Use**
   The verifiable exchange of narwhal tusks, at times alluded to as "white gold," essentially affects the animals and their natural surroundings. We will talk about the historical backdrop of the narwhal tusk exchange, its ramifications, and contemporary protection endeavors.

3. **The Narwhal Tusk in Contemporary Society**

Today, narwhal tusks are not just valued for their social and verifiable importance yet in addition face moral contemplations. This segment will analyze the contemporary purposes and discussions encompassing narwhal tusks, remembering their presence for workmanship, ancient rarities, and the market.

IV. Protection and Conservation

1. **Dangers to Narwhals**
   Narwhals face a scope of dangers, from environmental change and natural surroundings misfortune to human exercises like delivery and hunting.
   We will investigate the preservation difficulties and expected ramifications for narwhals and their tusks.

2. **Legitimate Assurances and Guidelines**
   Peaceful accords and guidelines have been set up to protect narwhals and their tusks. This part will give an outline of these lawful securities and the actions taken to battle unlawful exchange.

3. **Moral Contemplations**

As the protection of narwhals acquires unmistakable quality, moral contemplations in regards to the safeguarding of their tusks come to the very front. We will examine the moral issues encompassing the exchange, assortment, and show of narwhal tusks.

V. The Fate of Narwhals and Their Entrancing Tusks

1. **Preservation Endeavors**
   The protection of narwhals and their tusks involves worldwide significance. We will investigate continuous protection drives, research tasks, and endeavors to alleviate the dangers confronting these amazing animals.

2. **Promising Exploration Bearings**
   Logical exploration on narwhals and their tusks keeps on advancing. This segment will inspect arising research regions, including the potential for cutting edge innovations to reveal new insight into the secrets of the tusk.

3. **Bringing issues to light**

The narrative of narwhals and their interesting tusks fills in as a convincing image of the delicacy of the Cold biological system. We will talk about how bringing issues to light can motivate activity to safeguard these special animals and their puzzling tusks.

9.4 A Narwhal-inspired Lullaby

In the peaceful profundities of the Cold Sea, where the frigid waters hold mysteries past creative mind, an animal of persona and marvel skims effortlessly. The narwhal, frequently alluded to as the "unicorns of the ocean," captivates with its rich structure and the long, spiraling tusk that reaches out from its head.

This narwhal-enlivened children's song is an expressive excursion, a recognition for these delicate goliaths of the Cold domain, while conjuring the serene sorcery of sleep time.

Underneath the tremendous field of the Cold sky, where the stars sparkle like precious stones, the narwhal's presence is felt. It moves with a tranquil effortlessness, its tusk sparkling like a brilliant signal in the twilight, a directing light to lead exhausted spirits into the hug of sleep. The narwhal's dance in the profundities is an expressive dance of serenity, an update that in the quietness of the evening, there is comfort and harmony.

As the narwhal crosses the profundities, underneath the quiet look of the polar ice, it conveys with it the reverberations of antiquated melodies. These are the tunes of the ocean, an ensemble of murmurs that reverberation through the submerged realm. In this ethereal domain, secrets and miracles entwine, offering a brief look into a reality where narwhals and stars share their radiant mysteries. The evening glow's touch, delicate and delicate, paints an embroidery of dreams that dance upon the waves.

The narwhal's tusk, a puzzle in itself, is a demonstration of the wonders that untruth concealed underneath the surface. Like a remnant of a famous time, it holds accounts of wizardry, mental fortitude, and the everlasting dance among light and shadow. It is an update that occasionally, the best ponders are hidden in effortlessness, ready to be disentangled by the people who hope against hope.

In the core of the Icy, where the waters run profound and time stops, narwhals stand as watchmen of the void. They move in elegant harmony, a case joined by a solid bond. Their tunes are a language of affection, a song that rises above the profundities and reverberates with the hearts of all who tune in. As sunsets and dreams take off, narwhals look after, their insight and effortlessness winding around a casing of wellbeing around sleeping spirits.

Among these delicate monsters, narwhal moms hold a unique spot. Their adoration is a power of nature, a directing light for their young in the immense scope of the Cold ocean. With delicate consideration, they support and safeguard, conferring intelligence that traverses ages. The narwhal's cradlesong is a mother's sweet refrain, a commitment that even in the most profound of waters, love will continuously track down its direction.

As the narwhal-propelled children's song tenderly blurs, it abandons a feeling of miracle and serenity. The narwhal, with its smooth presence and entrancing tusk, has turned into an image of the enchanted that dwells underneath the waves. This children's song is an encouragement to dream, to relinquish stresses and embrace the secrets that anticipate in the profundities of the ocean.

Similarly as the narwhal directs its unit through the Icy waters, let this cradlesong guide you into a universe of dreams, where the miracles of the sea unfurl in the entirety of their grand quality.

Chapter 10

The Svalbard Siren's Aria

In the freezing scope of the Icy Sea, settled in the midst of ice-covered fjords and distant archipelagos, lies a position of charm and secret - Svalbard. This remote, barren, but hauntingly lovely locale has for some time been the subject of interest for researchers, pilgrims, and travelers. Nonetheless, lately, it has gathered consideration for an out and out various and baffling explanation - the Svalbard Alarm's Aria.

The Svalbard Alarm's Aria is a secretive peculiarity that has left researchers and specialists puzzled. Portrayed by powerful sounds reverberation underneath the frigid waters, enthralling the creative mind and starting a great many hypotheses and hypotheses. These confounding tunes, portrayed as both tormenting and wonderful, have perplexed established researchers, prompting different endeavors to make sense of their starting point and importance. This article means to dive profound into the core of this riddle, investigating the set of experiences, speculations, and logical examinations encompassing the Svalbard Alarm's Aria, with an end goal to comprehend the mysteries concealed underneath the Icy ice.

The Charming Setting: Svalbard

Svalbard, a Norwegian archipelago in the Cold Sea, is a place that is known for limits. It is perhaps of the coldest possessed put on The planet, with its capital, Longyearbyen, encountering polar night for a while every year. The archipelago's extraordinary geology and cruel environment make it an ideal setting for the strange peculiarity known as the Svalbard Alarm's Aria.

The Svalbard archipelago comprises of various islands, the biggest of which is Spitsbergen. It is here, in the midst of transcending ice sheets, desolate tundras, and cold waters, that the Alarm's Aria has been most often detailed. The disengagement and devastation of this district just add to the demeanor of persona encompassing the peculiarity.

Authentic Records

Reports of abnormal, ghostly sounds reverberating from the profundities of Svalbard's frosty waters date back a few centuries. The native Sámi individuals, who have possessed the locale for a really long time, have stories of these baffling sounds in their oral customs. Early European wayfarers and whalers likewise reported their encounters with the peculiarity.

One of the earliest recorded accounts is from a seventeenth century Dutch whaling campaign. Commander Willem Barentsz, an accomplished pioneer, wrote in his diary about hearing "charming tunes" underneath the waves close to the archipelago. These records, notwithstanding, were in many cases excused as the result of disengagement, unforgiving circumstances, and the overactive minds of mariners and voyagers.

In the cutting edge period, the peculiarity came to worldwide consideration through a progression of endeavors and logical examinations directed in the twentieth 100 years. The expression "Svalbard Alarm's Aria" was begat by a Norwegian sea life scholar, Dr. Elin Bjørnsson, who drove an undertaking to concentrate on the sounds in the mid 1970s. Her group's discoveries, which were distributed in a progression of logical diaries, made the way for additional request and interest.

Attributes of the Alarm's Aria

The Svalbard Alarm's Aria is portrayed by its particular and strange highlights, which put it aside from other submerged sounds and peculiarities. These highlights have just extended the secret and prompted a heap of hypotheses and hypotheses about its starting point and importance:

Ethereal Songs: The most characterizing part of the Alarm's Aria is the hauntingly lovely tunes that have been depicted by the individuals who have encountered it. Witnesses frequently use words like "ethereal," "extraordinary," and "charming" to depict the music that radiates from the profundities.

Shifted Sytheses: The songs are not reliable and seem to change after some time. A few reports propose that the sounds follow an example, while others depict irregular changes in tone, pitch, and musicality. Some have compared it to a continually developing orchestra.

Submerged Beginning: The sounds start from submerged, profound inside the frosty fjords and channels of Svalbard. They appear to resonate through the frigid waters, making a frightful, practically extraordinary air.

Occasional Varieties: The Alarm's Aria is definitely not a steady presence, and it has all the earmarks of being more conspicuous during explicit seasons, especially in the colder time of year and late-winter. This occasional variety has driven specialists to think about natural elements as a potential reason.

Hypotheses and Theories

The Svalbard Alarm's Aria has propelled a plenty of hypotheses and theories. Researchers, specialists, and aficionados the same have proposed different clarifications, each with its own extraordinary point of view on the puzzler. While none of these speculations can be absolutely demonstrated at this stage, they shed light on the assorted methodologies taken to grasp this puzzling peculiarity.

Geographical Action: One hypothesis sets that topographical action, for example, submerged volcanoes or moving structural plates, might be answerable for the sounds. These normal cycles could make vibrations that reverberate through the frosty waters, delivering the sweet tones.

Marine Life: Another speculation recommends that the sounds could be delivered by marine life, like submerged types of fish, scavangers, or even whales. These animals might be speaking with each other through complex vocalizations, which, when heard by people, are seen as a charming tune.

Cold Development: Svalbard is home to immense icy masses that are continually moving. A few scientists have recommended that the development of frigid ice could deliver sounds and vibrations that reverberation through the fjords, making the Alarm's Aria.

Electromagnetic Impedance: A later hypothesis sets that electromagnetic obstruction or uncommon attractive fields in the district could be liable for the peculiarity. These irregularities could influence the way of behaving of submerged minerals or rocks, delivering the particular sounds.

Barometrical Circumstances: Changes in air conditions, for example, temperature reversals or explicit breeze designs, have additionally been considered as expected causes. These climatic elements might impact the way strong goes through the Icy climate.

Legends and Fantasy: A few lovers propose that the Alarm's Aria is attached to neighborhood old stories and fantasies. In Nordic and Sámi legends, there are accounts of captivating ocean animals that utilization their melodies to draw mariners to their destruction. The peculiarity might be a cutting edge indication of these old stories.

Logical Examinations

While the Svalbard Alarm's Aria stays a secret, it has not gotten away from the consideration of established researchers. Throughout the long term, a few exploration campaigns and studies have been led to disentangle the mystery. These endeavors have utilized various strategies and advancements to grasp the starting points of the sounds.

Submerged Acoustics: Analysts have sent submerged listening gadgets and hydrophones to catch and break down the sounds. These instruments have given important information on the frequencies, examples, and starting points of the songs.

Seismic Examinations: Seismic sensors have been utilized to screen land action in the district. These sensors can distinguish structural developments, volcanic emissions, and other possible wellsprings of the sounds.

Sea life Science: Sea life scholars have led investigations to decide whether the sounds might be connected to explicit marine species. This includes following the relocation and conduct of fish, whales, and other submerged animals nearby.

Glaciology: Specialists in glaciology have analyzed the development and attributes of frosty ice in the locale. They intend to decide whether the sounds could be related with frosty exercises.

Attractive and Environmental Examinations: Researchers have analyzed the attractive and climatic circumstances in Svalbard to distinguish any oddities that could add to the peculiarity.

Results and Progressing Exploration

In spite of various examinations and studies, the starting points of the Svalbard Alarm's Aria stay subtle. A few specialists have proposed multi-layered clarifications, recommending that numerous variables might add to the peculiarity. For instance, the mix of cold development and marine life collaborations could make the particular tunes.

One ongoing idea in the examination is that the Alarm's Aria seems, by all accounts, to be attached to the novel natural states of Svalbard. The cold waters, the presence of glacial masses, and the occasional varieties all assume a part in molding this puzzling soundscape. Nonetheless, understanding the exact instruments and causes is a complicated and progressing try.

The Alarm's Aria keeps on being a subject of interest and interest for both mainstream researchers and the overall population. Interest in the peculiarity has prompted an expansion in the travel industry to Svalbard, with guests expecting to encounter the ethereal tunes for themselves. This, thusly, has raised worries about the effect of expanded human movement on the locale's delicate environment.

10.1 Introduction to Svalbard

Settled inside the Icy Circle, Svalbard is an archipelago covered in secret and miracle, frequently alluded to as the "last stop before the North Pole." This distant domain, situated in the high Icy locale, is portrayed by its obvious, frosty scenes, a rich history of investigation and asset double-dealing, and a remarkable mix of regular magnificence and testing everyday environments. With a set of experiences profoundly interlaced with polar investigation, logical examination, and worldwide participation, Svalbard has arisen as an image of our getting through interest with the furthest reaches of the world and the critical worldwide issues encompassing environmental change and asset the executives. In this article, we will leave on an excursion to find the marvels and intricacies of Svalbard, acquainting perusers with the archipelago's geology, history, culture, and its cutting edge job in resolving basic issues in the Cold.

Topography and Area

Svalbard is an archipelago arranged in the Cold Sea, around halfway between central area Norway and the North Pole. It lies around 700 kilometers (435 miles) north of the Norwegian central area and is many times thought about a piece of the Realm of Norway. The archipelago contains various islands, the biggest of which is Spitsbergen (Svalbard in Norwegian), trailed by Nordaustlandet, Edgeøya, Barentsøya, and numerous others. The all out land area of Svalbard covers around 61,000 square kilometers (23,600 square miles), making it one of the biggest expanses of land in the high Cold.

Svalbard's one of a kind topography is portrayed by its tough mountain ranges, tremendous ice sheets, and profound fjords. The archipelago is fundamentally covered by ice and snow, with more than 60% of its body of land covered by ice sheets. The unforgiving environment, with long, dull winters and generally cool summers, makes Svalbard perhaps of the most outrageous put on Earth to possess. The Cold

Sea encompasses the archipelago, and ocean ice is a typical component, especially during the long cold weather months.

History of Investigation

The historical backdrop of Svalbard is intently attached to the soul of polar investigation. Its disclosure can be followed back to the twelfth century when Norse adventures referenced "Svalbarð" (signifying "cold edge" or "cold coast"), alluding to this freezing and fruitless land. In any case, it was only after the seventeenth century that the archipelago started to be effectively investigated and colonized.

The Dutchman Willem Barents is frequently credited with the main kept revelation of Svalbard in 1596, during his journey to track down the Upper east Entry. Barents and his team endure a colder time of year on the island of Bear (presently Bjørnøya) and abandoned records of their excursion.

Svalbard turned into a center for whaling and seal hunting in the seventeenth and eighteenth hundreds of years, with different European countries laying out settlements and taking advantage of the rich marine assets. The archipelago was likewise a focal point for early Icy wayfarers, remembering the English Regal Naval force's undertakings for the nineteenth 100 years, drove by pioneers like Sir John Ross and Sir William Repel.

The Settlement of Svalbard

The late nineteenth and mid twentieth hundreds of years saw expanded worldwide interest in Svalbard, as countries competed for control and admittance to its significant normal assets, especially coal. To forestall struggle and lay out a system for collaboration, the Svalbard Settlement was endorsed in 1920 and came into force in 1925. This settlement perceived Norwegian power over the archipelago while guaranteeing that other signatory countries reserved the option to participate in business exercises, including mining, fishing, and logical examination, on an equivalent premise.

The Svalbard Settlement, otherwise called the Spitsbergen Arrangement, is much of the time proclaimed as one of the earliest peaceful accords for neutralization and the advancement of logical exploration in a far off district. It made a novel administration model for Svalbard, making it a worldwide region where Norwegian regulation applies yet with specific exclusions and privileges for residents of settlement signatory countries. This deal system actually oversees the archipelago today and has added to Svalbard's worldwide significance as a site for logical exploration and ecological participation.

Present day Socioeconomics and Networks

Notwithstanding its brutal environment and distant area, Svalbard is home to a little yet different populace. The biggest settlement and managerial focus of the archipelago is Longyearbyen, situated on Spitsbergen. Other huge settlements incorporate Barentsburg (a Russian coal-mining town), Ny-Ålesund (an exploration town), and a few more modest networks.

Longyearbyen, with its populace of around 2,400 occupants, is the business, instructive, and social center of Svalbard. It houses the Legislative leader of Svalbard's workplaces, the College Place in Svalbard (UNIS), and different exploration establishments, including the Svalbard Worldwide Seed Vault, a pivotal office for safeguarding plant hereditary variety.

The socioeconomics of Svalbard are worldwide in nature, with occupants hailing from different nations. While Norwegians make up the biggest part of the populace, occupants additionally come from Russia, Sweden, Denmark, and different countries. The exceptional administration design of Svalbard considers residents of these nations to live and work in the archipelago without requiring a proper visa, making it an appealing objective for the two scientists and explorers.

Difficulties and Amazing open doors

Svalbard's far off area, testing environment, and restricted foundation present various difficulties for the people who decide to live and work in the archipelago. The absolute most major problems include:

Environmental Change: The Cold is one of the locales generally impacted by environmental change, and Svalbard is no exemption.

Climbing temperatures, softening ice, and moving weather conditions significantly affect the climate, natural life, and human networks in the archipelago.

Ecological Preservation: Svalbard is home to assorted and extraordinary biological systems, including Icy greenery. Ecological preservation endeavors are basic to safeguard the district's fragile equilibrium even with expanding human exercises.

Asset The executives: The double-dealing of normal assets, especially coal mining and fishing, has been a critical piece of Svalbard's set of experiences. Offsetting monetary interests with supportability and ecological worries is a continuous test.

Foundation and Availability: The archipelago's restricted framework, including transportation and correspondence organizations, presents strategic difficulties. Be that as it may, further developing these offices can upgrade research abilities and by and large day to day environments.

Cold Exploration: Svalbard's essential area has made it a significant community for Icy examination. Progressing concentrates on environmental change, glaciology, and biological systems are urgent for figuring out worldwide ecological changes.

The Svalbard Worldwide Seed Vault

One of the most popular highlights of Svalbard is the Svalbard Worldwide Seed Vault, frequently alluded to as the "Judgment day Vault." Situated in a protected office inside a mountain on Spitsbergen, the seed vault fills in as a reinforcement storeroom for seeds from around the world. Its essential mission is to shield the hereditary variety of significant food crops in case of a worldwide fiasco, like cataclysmic events, war, or environment related occasions.

The seed vault stores seeds from virtually every nation, making it an image of worldwide participation and the significance of protecting farming biodiversity. It has been intended to endure many likely dangers and is overseen by the Norwegian government as a team with the

Worldwide Yield Variety Trust and the Food and Farming Association (FAO) of the Unified Countries.

The Eventual fate of Svalbard

As the world wrestles with major problems, for example, environmental change, asset the board, and the conservation of biodiversity, Svalbard takes on another degree of importance. Its special administration model, far off area, and progressing research exercises make it a central participant in tending to these worldwide difficulties.

Svalbard's future holds the commitment of proceeded with logical disclosure, global cooperation, and mindful asset the board. It fills in as an image of our persevering through interest with the World's polar districts and the basic job they play in the planet's biological equilibrium. As we push ahead, it is crucial for balance the archipelago's rich history of investigation and asset double-dealing with a guarantee to natural stewardship and supportability, guaranteeing that Svalbard's inheritance is one of enduring worth to both the neighborhood local area and the worldwide populace.

10.2 The Unique Wildlife of Svalbard

Settled inside the Cold Circle, Svalbard is an unmistakable and unforgiving archipelago set apart by frosty scenes and outrageous weather patterns. Regardless of its considerable climate, Svalbard is home to a shockingly different scope of natural life. This novel biological system has adjusted to flourish in quite possibly of the cruelest climate on The planet. In this article, we will investigate the wonderful animals that call Svalbard home, revealing insight into their transformations, ways of behaving, and the difficulties they face in a quickly changing Cold scene.

Cold Fox (Vulpes lagopus)

The Icy fox, otherwise called the polar fox, is a notable types of the Icy and an expert of variation to cold conditions. These little vertebrates show a few striking elements that assist them with getting by in the unforgiving states of Svalbard:

Thick Fur: Cold foxes have a thick, complex coat that assists them with holding body heat. Their fur changes tone with the seasons, giving successful cover against the blanketed scenes. In winter, their fur is white, while in summer, it becomes brown or dark.

Conduct Variations: To moderate energy during unforgiving winters, Cold foxes are known to dig tunnels and make complex underground caves. These lairs act as haven from the cold, giving a stable microclimate to raising their young.

Hunting Techniques: Cold foxes fundamentally feed on little vertebrates, birds, and fish. They are crafty trackers and foragers, frequently following polar bears and rummaging their kills. This conduct permits them to get to high-energy food sources.

Polar Bear (Ursus maritimus)

The polar bear, frequently alluded to as the "Ruler of the Cold," is the biggest land meat eater on The planet. These dominant hunters are extraordinarily adjusted to the freezing Icy climate, with transformations, for example,

Protecting Fur: Polar bears have a thick layer of lard underneath their fur that gives protection and assists them with remaining warm in freezing waters. Their fur seems white however is really clear.

Swimming Ability: Polar bears serious areas of strength for are, equipped for covering significant distances looking for seals and other prey. They are known to cover distances of many kilometers in the vast sea, depending on their strong appendages and webbed paws.

Ocean Ice Reliance: Polar bears principally chase seals, and their endurance is firmly connected to the accessibility of ocean ice. They use ocean ice as stages from which to trap seals that surface to relax.

Protection Concerns: Environmental change represents a huge danger to polar bears. As the Icy ocean ice contracts because of climbing temperatures, polar bears are compelled to go more noteworthy distances to find food, prompting diminished body condition and lower proliferation rates.

Svalbard Reindeer (Rangifer tarandus platyrhynchus)

The Svalbard reindeer is a subspecies of the reindeer local to the archipelago. These creatures show a few transformations to life in the Icy tundra:

Little Size: Svalbard reindeer are more modest than their central area family members, which is a transformation that assists them with moderating energy and lessen heat misfortune in the chilly climate.

Thick Fur and Layered Coat: They have a thick fur garment and an underlayer of fleece that protects them from the super virus. In winter, their fur becomes lighter in variety.

Taking care of Methodologies: Svalbard reindeer principally eat on Cold vegetation like greeneries, lichens, and grasses. They utilize their hooves to dig through snow to get to food throughout the cold weather months.

Social Design: These reindeer will generally shape more modest crowds, which can incorporate people of different ages. Their social design is somewhat adaptable, permitting them to adjust to evolving conditions.

Icy Bird Species

Svalbard is home to an assortment of Icy bird species that variety on the archipelago during the short summer season. A few prominent models include:

Icy Tern (Sterna paradisaea): Known for its significant distance movement, the Cold tern ventures out from the Icy to the Antarctic and back, covering the longest relocation course of any bird.

Normal Eider (Somateria mollissima): These enormous, ocean duck species are renowned for their down feathers, which are utilized to protect settles and are exceptionally pursued by people for down-filled items.

Ivory Gull (Pagophila eburnea): A strikingly white bird, the ivory gull is an image of the Icy and is exceptionally adjusted to cold conditions.

Little Auk (alle): A little seabird that homes in rough hole, little auks are known for their huge reproducing provinces in Svalbard.

Marine Life

Svalbard's encompassing waters are overflowing with marine life, regardless of the super virus. A portion of the marine species that occupy the locale include:

Ringed Seal (Pusa hispida): This little seal species is profoundly adjusted to Icy circumstances and is known for its ring-like markings on its jacket. They make breathing openings in the ocean ice and are an essential prey animal varieties for polar bears.

Icy Cod (Boreogadus saida): These little, chilly water fish assume a urgent part in the Cold food web and are an essential food hotspot for different marine hunters.

Beluga Whale (Delphinapterus leucas): The beluga is a particular white whale known for its echolocation capacities. These marine vertebrates are in many cases found in the Icy waters encompassing Svalbard.

Walrus (Odobenus rosmarus): Walruses are huge, tusked marine well evolved creatures that are known to pull out on the ocean ice and waterfront regions. They feed on shellfishes and other base dwelling life forms.

Difficulties and Protection

The novel untamed life of Svalbard faces a scope of difficulties, essentially because of the effects of environmental change and human exercises. A portion of the key worries include:

Environmental Change: Increasing temperatures and softening ocean ice are influencing the territories and prey accessibility for species like polar bears. Changes in ice designs likewise influence seal populaces, an essential food hotspot for polar bears.

Expanded Human Movement: Developing the travel industry and logical exploration exercises in Svalbard can prompt aggravations of untamed life, territory corruption, and expanded dangers of oil slicks from transportation.

Intrusive Species: The presentation of non-local species represents a danger to the delicate Cold environments. The reindeer, for instance, have encountered disturbances right at home because of the presence of non-local plant species.

Preservation Endeavors: Different global and public endeavors are in progress to address these difficulties. These incorporate preservation measures for polar bears, safeguarded regions for seabird provinces, and rules for mindful the travel industry.

10.3 Conservation Efforts in the Arctic

The Cold, one of the world's last outskirts, is home to extraordinary biological systems and natural life that have adjusted to its unforgiving and freezing conditions over centuries. Notwithstanding, environmental change, contamination, and expanded human exercises are presenting huge dangers to this flawless climate. Subsequently, preservation endeavors in the Icy have acquired expanding significance as of late. In this article, we will investigate the difficulties confronting the Cold, the drives and techniques pointed toward safeguarding its sensitive biological systems, and the global joint effort important to safeguard this crucial area.

The Difficulties

The Cold district faces a huge number of difficulties, fundamentally determined by environmental change and human exercises. These difficulties include:

Dissolving Ocean Ice: Cold ocean ice is contracting at a disturbing rate because of increasing worldwide temperatures. The deficiency of ocean ice influences polar bears, seals, and other ice-subordinate species, undermining their endurance.

Dangers to Marine Life: Contamination, overfishing, and expanded transportation traffic in the Icy Sea can upset marine biological systems and adversely influence species like whales, seals, and seabirds.

Permafrost Defrost: The defrosting of permafrost discharges ozone depleting substances into the air, compounding an Earth-wide temperature boost and making a criticism circle that further speeds up environmental change.

Intrusive Species: The presentation of non-local species represents a danger to the Cold's one of a kind biodiversity, as these species can outcompete and uproot local widely varied vegetation.

Contamination: Defilement from oil slicks, plastic waste, and poisons can lastingly affect Icy biological systems, as the cool climate can dial back the breakdown of these materials.

Expanded Human Action: Growing human exercises, including the travel industry, transportation, and asset extraction, can upset natural life and their territories, prompting environment corruption and possible struggles with neighborhood networks.

Worldwide Protection Endeavors

Tending to the difficulties confronting the Cold requires cooperative endeavors at the global level. Different associations, settlements, and arrangements have been laid out to safeguard this weak district and its novel environments:

The Icy Gathering: Shaped in 1996, the Icy Committee is an intergovernmental discussion for Icy states, native people groups, and different partners to address natural and practical advancement issues in the district. It centers around examination, observing, and security of the Icy climate.

The Antarctic Deal: While basically centered around the Antarctic locale, the Antarctic Settlement Framework plays likewise had an impact in safeguarding the Cold. It starts a trend for worldwide participation in the administration and preservation of a polar locale.

The Svalbard Settlement: As referenced in a past article, the Svalbard Deal (Spitsbergen Arrangement) controls exercises in the Svalbard archipelago, permitting signatory countries to participate in logical examination and asset the executives while regarding preservation and natural security.

The Show for the Protection of Antarctic Marine Living Assets (CCAMLR): Despite the fact that its essential spotlight is on the Southern Sea, CCAMLR fills in as a model for global collaboration in the guideline of business fisheries, which could be applied to the Cold to deal with the double-dealing of living assets.

The Global Sea Association (IMO): The IMO is liable for managing worldwide transportation, remembering for the Icy. Its guidelines expect to decrease the ecological effect of transportation, forestall oil slicks, and safeguard marine life.

The Cold Marine Transportation Evaluation (AMSA): The AMSA, led by the Icy Board, gave proposals and rules to more secure and all the more harmless to the ecosystem delivering rehearses in the Icy.

The Focal Cold Sea Fisheries Understanding: In 2018, a noteworthy arrangement was reached among a few countries lining the focal Icy Sea to forestall unregulated fishing in this recently open locale, showing a proactive way to deal with preservation.

Preservation Drives

While peaceful accords give a structure to preservation, different associations and drives are effectively taken part in endeavors to safeguard the Icy. A few prominent drives include:

Icy Safeguarded Regions: The foundation of marine safeguarded regions and preservation zones in the Icy is essential for defending marine life and territories. These regions expect to restrict human exercises and give places of refuge to species undermined by environmental change and overfishing.

Native Stewardship: Native people group have for quite some time been stewards of the Cold climate. Cooperative endeavors with these networks are fundamental for supportable asset the board and the assurance of natural life.

Environment Exploration and Checking: Predictable and extensive information on Icy environmental change are significant for figuring out its effects and directing protection endeavors. Continuous examination and observing give fundamental data to policymakers and researchers.

Advancing Manageable Practices: Associations and states are advancing reasonable the travel industry and dependable practices in the Cold, expecting to lessen the ecological impression of human exercises.

Untamed life Insurance: Protection associations are attempting to safeguard famous Cold species, like polar bears and seals, by resolving issues like natural surroundings conservation, lessening human-untamed life clashes, and supporting recovery endeavors.

Environment Alleviation: Peaceful accords, for example, the Paris Understanding, expect to moderate worldwide environmental change, which is central to safeguarding the Cold. Diminishing ozone harming substance emanations can dial back the liquefying of ocean ice and the warming of the Cold.

The Job of Innovation

Progresses in innovation are assuming a basic part in Icy protection endeavors. Remote detecting, satellite symbolism, and submerged mechanical technology empower scientists to screen changes in the Icy climate and study natural life without causing aggravations. Drones and independent vehicles can give important information to preservation drives, for example, evaluating the soundness of ocean ice or following creature populaces.

Moreover, innovation decreases the natural effect of human exercises in the Icy. For instance, cleaner and more proficient transportation advances can limit the gamble of oil slicks and lessen discharges, while developments in squander the executives and environmentally friendly power frameworks support more manageable practices in the district.

Difficulties and Future Bearings

Preservation endeavors in the Icy are faced by a scope of difficulties. A portion of the key obstacles include:

Environmental Change: Easing back the pace of environmental change is vital for Icy protection. The liquefying of ocean ice, permafrost defrost, and warming temperatures have sweeping ramifications for the locale's environments.

Adjusting Preservation and Improvement: Finding some kind of harmony between safeguarding the Icy and it is trying to empower reasonable monetary turn of events. Asset extraction, the travel industry, and delivery are imperative for a few Icy people group yet should be made do in light of ecological worries.

Subsidizing and Assets: Preservation drives in the Icy require significant financing and assets. Getting these assets, especially for remote and strategically testing projects, can be a huge impediment.

Cross-Boundary Joint effort: Viable protection in the Cold relies upon global participation. Clashing public interests, political pressures, and the test of adjusting different partners can thwart progress.

As the Cold keeps on going through quick changes, the eventual fate of its preservation will rely upon our capacity to address these difficulties and work on the whole to safeguard this delicate and fundamental environment. Peaceful accords, creative innovation, and a developing consciousness of the significance of the Cold to worldwide environment and biodiversity are adding to the continuous endeavors to defend this special and weak locale. In doing as such, we can safeguard the Icy's perfect wild for people in the future and keep up with its basic job in the World's environment framework.

10.4 A Svalbard-inspired Lullaby

In the place where there is ice and dreams, where the Icy breezes murmur mysteries of the frozen world, there exists a spot like no other: Svalbard. This distant archipelago, arranged in the Icy Sea, catches the hearts and psyches of all who adventure into its captivating hug. Its tough, snow-shrouded scenes, polar bears that wander the ice, and the ethereal dance of Aurora Borealis in the colder time of year sky make Svalbard a position of marvel and secret. It's a land where time appears to stop, where the limits among the real world and dream obscure. This is the motivation for a Svalbard-propelled bedtime song, a delicate tune that winds around together the wizardry and magnificence of this remote corner of the world.

As the sun plunges beneath the skyline, projecting a delicate, blushing tint across the snow-shrouded fields, maybe Svalbard herself is murmuring to her occupants, encouraging them to discover a sense of reconciliation in the serene haziness of the polar evening. The children's song starts with a depiction of the Cold scene. The initial sections illustrate the snow-covered mountains, frigid fjords, and the always present quietness that wraps the archipelago. It discusses the captivating play of light and shadow on the snow, an indication of the consistently changing nature of this frozen world.

"In the place that is known for ice and dreams, where the polar breezes tenderly murmur, where the mountains contact the sky and the fjords embrace the ocean, in Svalbard's immortal evening, let your soul wander aimlessly. In the place that is known for unending snow, where Aurora Borealis captivate the sky, where the polar bears discreetly wander and the icy masses stand tall, in Svalbard's peaceful hug, may your fantasies take off."

The bedtime song then presents the glorious polar bear, an image of Svalbard's wild and untamed nature. These grand animals, all around adjusted to life in the unforgiving Cold climate, summon both apprehension and wonder.

The verses depict their sluggish, elegant developments over the ice, a sign of the fragile equilibrium of life in this freezing domain.

"Among the snow and ice, where the polar bears rule, with their fur so unadulterated and white, they're an image of this land. In Svalbard's quiet world, may you track down strength and effortlessness. As the polar bears meander the ice, in the Icy's wide hug."

The cradlesong then, at that point, directs concentration toward the supernatural peculiarity graces the Icy sky - Aurora Borealis. The shining draperies of green, purple, and blue dance in the night sky, projecting a supernatural sparkle over the frozen scenes. The verses discuss the aurora borealis as a divine light show that touches off the creative mind and fills the heart with amazement.

"At the point when the night sky wakes up, with Aurora Borealis' delicate moan, as they dance and shine splendid, in the Cold's frozen evening. In Svalbard's mysterious shine, may your fantasies take off and develop. With the auroras' delicate beauty, let your soul track down its place."

As the cradlesong proceeds, it investigates the topic of strength and flexibility, characteristics that are fundamental for endurance in the brutal Icy environment. The verses underscore the significance of tracking down strength even with difficulty, drawing motivation from the tough scenes and the diligence of the vegetation that call Svalbard home.

"In the place that is known for ice and snow, where the tundra sprouts and develops, where life figures out how to flourish, with each challenge it will endeavor. In Svalbard's unfaltering heart, may you track down the solidarity to begin. With the tundra's peaceful may, let your fantasies take off."

The children's song then, at that point, proceeds, zeroing in on the human presence in Svalbard. The archipelago is home to a little however strong local area, where individuals reside and work as one with the outrageous climate. The verses praise the soul of investigation and the persevering through human association with this remote corner of the world.

"In the place that is known for ice and dreams, where the Cold spirits sparkle, where individuals track down their direction, in Svalbard's unending day. In the human stories told, may you track down your endearing personality. With individuals' cold love, let your fantasies take off above."

Svalbard isn't just a position of charm yet additionally a demonstration of the significance of safeguarding our planet's delicate environments. The bedtime song's next refrains pass on the message of natural stewardship and the need to safeguard this immaculate wild for people in the future.

"In the place that is known for ice and dreams, where nature's magnificence generally radiates, where we should safeguard and mind, for the Icy's wild, we should bear. In Svalbard's delicate effortlessness, let us track down our legitimate spot. With the world we should join together, to safeguard this Cold light."

The cradlesong arrives at its determination with a last message of trust and love. It urges the audience to embrace the sorcery of Svalbard and convey it in their souls, to track down motivation in the magnificence of the world, and to dream of a superior, more amicable future for all.

"In the place that is known for ice and dreams, where Svalbard's sorcery at any point sparkles, where love and trust join together, in the Icy's delicate light. In Svalbard's delicate hold, may your fantasies take off and strong. With the world's adoring may, may we make everything right."

As the cradlesong blurs into the calm of the Cold evening, it abandons a feeling of marvel and charm, similar as the land that roused it. Svalbard's immortal excellence, its wild occupants, and the always changing play of light and shadow keep on dazzling the hearts of the individuals who try to wander into this frozen domain. The Svalbard-roused children's song fills in as a sign of the wizardry and secret that can be tracked down in even the most remote and testing corners of our reality, and the significance of safeguarding these spots for people in the future to treasure and secure.

Chapter 11

Composing Arctic Lullabies

The presentation sets the stage, offering a brief look into the charming universe of Cold bedtime songs. It gives setting on the meaning of these tunes and their association with the Icy area's different native societies, unmistakable scenes, and dynamic natural life. The part likewise frames the reason, degree, technique, and construction of the exposition, laying out an unmistakable guide for the peruser's excursion.

The Icy Locale: An Outline:

This part lays out a striking representation of the Icy, incorporating its geological elements, outrageous environment, and its crucial job as home to a mosaic of native people groups. It digs into the subtleties of Cold topography, featuring its sweeping ice-shrouded spreads, bone chilling environment, and unmistakable biological systems. Furthermore, it presents the different native networks that have flourished in this difficult climate for ages, underlining their well established association with the land and ocean.

Bedtime songs: An All inclusive Language:

Here, the all inclusive nature of children's songs is investigated, rising above social and geological limits. The segment enlightens the force of children's songs in mitigating and encouraging babies, decreasing pressure, and working with rest. It underlines their social importance as vessels for sending information, customs, and language starting with one age then onto the next, making them a vital string in the texture of native societies around the world.

Cold Cradlesongs: A Social Embroidery:

This portion drenches the peruser in the different woven artwork of Cold bedtime songs, highlighting the extraordinary commitments of native networks like the Inuit, Sámi, Aleut, Alutiiq, Chukchi, and Evenki. Each culture's bedtime songs are analyzed, offering bits of knowledge into their particular styles, subjects, and social settings. From the delicate songs of Inuit cradlesongs to the respectful impressions of Sámi bedtime songs, this part praises the rich variety inside Icy melodic practices.

Songs from the North: Instruments and Vocal Methods:

This segment gives a top to bottom investigation of the melodic components that shape Cold children's songs.

It presents conventional Cold instruments and vocal methods, revealing insight into the particular sounds that imbue these songs with their special person. The combination of conventional and contemporary melodic components is additionally investigated, exhibiting how Cold cradlesongs adjust and advance over the long run.

The Icy Scene in Music:

Diving into the core of Cold motivation, this segment distinctively depicts the entrancing scenes that act as the scenery for these bedtime songs. From the frigid scopes to the ethereal dance of Aurora Borealis, the Cold climate meshes itself into the actual texture of these tunes. The segment additionally praises the rich biodiversity of the district, including its famous natural life and their significant effect on Cold music.

Environmentalism and Activism in Icy Cradlesongs:

This portion resolves the major problems of environmental change and ecological activism in the Cold setting. It investigates how Cold bedtime songs have turned into a strong vehicle for communicating worries about the changing climate and the flexibility of native networks notwithstanding these difficulties. The voices of native activists are featured, displaying their part in the worldwide natural development.

Variation and Development of Icy Children's songs:

This segment carries the account into the current day, analyzing how Icy bedtime songs proceed to develop and adjust. It investigates present day understandings of these songs, as well as multifaceted joint efforts that reinvigorate customary tunes. The endeavors to save and advance Icy melodic legacy are additionally highlighted, underscoring the persevering through significance of these bedtime songs in contemporary society.

11.1 The Creative Process

The inventive flow is a strange and enamoring venture that fills human development and creative articulation. It is a sensitive dance among motivation and execution, a journey into the profundities of the human psyche, and a powerful power that has formed our reality since forever ago. In this investigation, we will dive into the complexities of the inventive flow, analyzing its stages, factors impacting it, and the job it plays in different parts of life, from craftsmanship and science to critical thinking and self-improvement.

1. **The Innovative flow Divulged**
1. **Motivation and Creative mind**

    At the core of the innovative strategy lies motivation, a flash that lights the creative mind. Motivation can emerge out of different sources: nature, feelings, encounters, or considerably other inventive works. It frequently strikes out of the blue, causing a surge of thoughts and conceivable outcomes. Creative mind, the capacity to frame mental pictures, is where this underlying motivation comes to fruition. It's a jungle gym where the brain investigates and builds new ideas, pictures, and stories.

2. **Brooding and Permeation**

    After the underlying eruption of motivation, numerous creatives experience a time of hatching. This is an apparently inactive stage during which the brain keeps on dealing with the thought underneath the surface. It's the subliminal's approach to permeating the thought, permitting it to develop and advance without the maker's immediate cognizant exertion. It is during this stage that apparently inconsequential encounters and data associate, bringing about original experiences.

3. **Enlightenment and Aha Minutes**

   The zenith of the inventive flow is frequently set apart by snapshots of enlightenment. These are the "aha" minutes when the arrangement, thought, or work of art takes a substantial structure. Maybe a light has been turned on, and the maker sees the way ahead. These minutes can be invigorating and some of the time incomprehensible, however they are the aftereffect of the brain's tireless work during the brooding stage.

4. **Confirmation and Refinement**

When the underlying idea has been enlightened, the innovative approach shifts toward confirmation and refinement. This stage includes assessing the thought's achievability, common sense, and its possible effect on the interest group. Makers test their ideas and make essential acclimations to guarantee that the eventual outcome or thought is all around organized and lined up with their unique vision.

II. Factors Impacting the Innovative flow

1. **Mental Elements**

   Stream Express: The condition of "stream" is described by complete retention in an imaginative errand, where the maker's expertise level and the test within reach are impeccably adjusted. Accomplishing stream can upgrade imagination and efficiency.

   Inspiration: Imagination frequently flourishes when people are naturally roused, driven by a certifiable energy for their work, instead of outside remunerations.

Mental Adaptability: The capacity to move viewpoints and think in whimsical ways is a vital part of the inventive flow. This includes breaking liberated from unbending idea designs.

2. **Ecological Variables**

Strong Climate: A sustaining and steady climate can give the essential consolation and assets for inventive undertakings. This might incorporate admittance to materials, time, and a local area of similar people.

Motivation and Openness: Openness to different encounters, societies, and thoughts can light the innovative flash. Travel, perusing, and openness to different artistic expressions can grow the psyche and give new points of view.

Space and Environment: The actual work area and its climate can fundamentally affect inventiveness. A climate that is helpful for fixation and unwinding can improve the innovative flow.

3. **Time and Tolerance**

Imagination frequently calls for investment and persistence. The inventive strategy isn't generally straight and can be dependent upon times of vulnerability and uncertainty. Showing restraint toward oneself and taking into consideration the vital hatching and refinement stages is fundamental for a fruitful imaginative result.

III. The Inventive approach in Various Fields

1. **Craftsmanship and Plan**

The imaginative innovative flow includes catching feelings, stories, and dynamic ideas in unmistakable structures. Craftsmen utilize their creative mind and abilities to change thoughts into artworks, figures, photos, and that's just the beginning.

The plan inventive strategy is fundamental in fields like visual communication, style, and modern plan. It centers around taking care of issues through stylish and useful arrangements.

2. **Science and Advancement**

   Logical disclosure frequently follows an inventive flow. Researchers figure out theories, direct examinations, and break down information to uncover new information and developments. Mechanical advancement depends on imagination to foster new items, administrations, and arrangements. Organizations frequently urge inventive reasoning to stay serious.

3. **Critical thinking and Decisive Reasoning**

Imaginative critical thinking includes breaking new ground to track down inventive answers for difficulties. This cycle is relevant in different regions, from business procedure to individual important choices.

Decisive reasoning, a firmly related process, empowers people to basically examine and assess data. It is a pivotal part of inventive critical thinking.

IV. Imagination and Self-improvement

1. **Self-Articulation and Character**

   Participating in the innovative flow permits people to articulate their thoughts and investigate their characters. It is a method for imparting one's contemplations, sentiments, and encounters with the world.

2. **Profound Therapy**

   Imagination can act as a strong source for feelings. Composing, painting, and other inventive exercises can help people cycle and delivery repressed feelings, giving profound alleviation and recuperating.

3. **Self-Disclosure**

The inventive approach frequently includes contemplation and self-revelation. By digging into one's viewpoints and feelings, people can acquire a more profound comprehension of themselves and their inward universes.

V. Conquering Difficulties in the Inventive flow

1. Imaginative Blocks

Imaginative blocks are normal obstacles experienced by craftsmen, scholars, and makers. These snapshots of stagnation can be disappointing, yet they are a characteristic piece of the interaction. Systems to defeat imaginative blocks incorporate transforming one's current circumstance, looking for new motivation, and enjoying reprieves.

2. Feeling of dread toward Disappointment

The feeling of dread toward disappointment can deaden innovative people. The innovative flow implies facing challenges, and embracing disappointment as a learning opportunity is fundamental. Rethinking disappointment as a venturing stone to progress can engage makers to push through dread.

3. Burnout

Creatives are defenseless against burnout because of the extraordinary mental and close to home requests of the interaction. To forestall burnout, makers should focus on taking care of oneself, put down stopping points, and consider times of rest and revival.

VI. The Advancement of the Inventive flow

1. Innovation's Effect

Progressions in innovation have extraordinarily affected the innovative strategy. Advanced devices, programming, and online stages have extended the opportunities for specialists, architects, and designers. They have additionally had an impact on the way creatives team up and share their work.

2. Globalization and Different Points of view

The interconnectedness of the cutting edge world has presented people to a great many societies and viewpoints. This globalization has improved the innovative flow by mixing it with assorted impacts and thoughts.

3. Interdisciplinary Methodologies

The limits between various fields of innovativeness are turning out to be progressively obscured. Interdisciplinary methodologies are encouraging development as makers draw motivation from a large number of sources and information spaces.

11.2 Collaborating with Arctic Researchers

The Cold district, with its amazing scenes, extraordinary biological systems, and basic significance notwithstanding environmental change, offers a variety of chances and difficulties for specialists. Teaming up with Cold analysts has become progressively crucial as we endeavor to comprehend and address the ecological, social, and international issues related with this area. In this investigation, we will dig into the meaning of Cold exploration, the intricacies of teaming up in such a remote and cruel climate, the multi-layered disciplines included, and the effect of these joint efforts on the fate of the Icy.

1. **The Meaning of Cold Exploration**
1. **Environmental Change and Natural Effect**
   The Cold is especially powerless against the impacts of environmental change, with temperatures increasing at over two times the worldwide normal. Cooperative examination endeavors are crucial for screen, record, and dissect the significant changes happening around here, including the contracting of ice sheets, adjustments in sea dissemination, and changes in untamed life living spaces.
2. **Remarkable Environments and Biodiversity**
   The Icy flaunts a different scope of environments and exceptional biodiversity. Cooperative exploration permits researchers to concentrate on the variations of Cold species and the natural associations inside this outrageous climate. Understanding

these frameworks can have sweeping ramifications for protection endeavors around the world.

3. **Social Conservation**

The Icy is home to various native networks, each with its own rich social legacy. Cooperative examination frequently includes working with these networks to safeguard their practices, information, and lifestyle while tending to the difficulties they face in an evolving Cold.

4. **International Significance**

The dissolving of Cold ice has opened up new open doors for asset investigation and delivery courses. Cooperative examination assumes a vital part in tending to global strategies, security concerns, and practical administration of Cold assets.

II. The Intricacies of Teaming up in the Cold

1. **Cruel Natural Circumstances**

The Icy presents an exceptional arrangement of difficulties, including outrageous cold, long periods of haziness, and the disengagement of remote examination stations. Specialists should adjust to these circumstances, which can be truly and intellectually requesting.

2. **Foundation and Strategies**

Moving scientists, hardware, and supplies to the Cold can be strategically difficult and costly. Cooperation frequently includes organizing the utilization of exploration vessels, airplane, and icebreakers to get to remote locales.

3. **Security and Wellbeing Contemplations**

The cruel Cold climate presents wellbeing and wellbeing dangers to specialists. These incorporate openness to outrageous cold, untamed life experiences, and the gamble of mishaps during hands on work. Cooperative endeavors should focus on wellbeing conventions and crisis reaction methodology.

4. Cross-Disciplinary Coordinated effort

Cold exploration frequently requires coordinated effort among researchers from different disciplines, including geologists, scholars, climatologists, and social researchers. Successful correspondence and the capacity to coordinate discoveries from assorted fields are fundamental for thorough exploration.

III. Disciplines Associated with Icy Exploration

1. Innate Sciences

Environment Science: Understanding the perplexing connections between the Cold environment and the worldwide environment framework is crucial to evaluating the results of environmental change.

Oceanography: Concentrating on the Icy Sea's physical and substance properties, including the impacts of liquefying ice, is indispensable for figuring out environment elements.

Science and Biology: Specialists concentrate on Icy untamed life, from polar bears to microorganisms, to evaluate the effect of ecological changes on the district's environments.

2. Sociologies

Human sciences: Social researchers work with native networks to concentrate on social changes, customs, and the effects of environmental change on these networks.

International relations: Cold analysts inspect worldwide relations, strategies, and arrangements administering the locale, tending to the complex international elements of the Icy.

Social science: Understanding the social and financial ramifications of environmental change and asset double-dealing in Icy people group is pivotal for feasible turn of events.

3. Innovation and Advancement

Remote Detecting: Trend setting innovation, including satellites and automated airborne vehicles (UAVs), is utilized to screen and gather information in far off Icy regions.

Information Examination: With tremendous measures of information produced, information researchers and experts assume a huge part in deciphering and removing important bits of knowledge.

IV. The Effect of Cooperative Cold Exploration

1. **Logical Revelations**

   Cooperative exploration in the Icy has prompted various notable logical disclosures, revealing insight into the locale's biological changes, the way of behaving of Icy species, and the elements of polar ice sheets. These revelations add to our more extensive comprehension of worldwide environment frameworks.

2. **Strategy and The board**

   Icy exploration has straightforwardly informed global approaches and settlements on environmental change, asset the board, and native privileges. Logical proof aides decision-production at the public and global levels, impacting economical turn of events and protection endeavors.

3. **Social Conservation**

   Joint effort with native networks has helped save their social legacy and conventional information. These organizations advance regard for native privileges and give a stage to tending to the remarkable difficulties these networks face.

4. **Instruction and Public Mindfulness**

Cold exploration coordinated efforts have instructive and public mindfulness parts, drawing in understudies, the overall population, and policymakers. Outreach drives assist with conveying the significance of Icy examination and motivate people in the future of researchers.

V. Difficulties and Future Contemplations

1. **Subsidizing and Assets**
   Supporting Cold exploration joint efforts requires steady financing and assets. Many tasks rely upon global participation and backing, making monetary steadiness a basic concern.

2. **Environmental Change Relief**
   The Icy is frequently portrayed as the "canary in the coal mineshaft" for environmental change. Successful joint effort is expected to address relief techniques and adjust to the progressions currently in progress.

3. **Native Commitment**
   Regarding the freedoms and information on native networks is fundamental in Cold exploration. Organizations with these networks ought to be additionally reinforced to guarantee fair support and direction.

4. **Innovation and Development**

Progressions in innovation are basic for conquering the difficulties of Cold examination. Analysts should keep on embracing advancement, from further developing information assortment methods to upgrading the security of hands on work.

11.3 Recording and Sharing the Lullabies

Cradlesongs, those delicate and relieving songs sung to solace and quiet babies, hold a treasured spot in the social practices of social orders all over the planet. Impossible for them to hush a youngster to rest, cradlesongs convey with them the heaviness of legacy, custom, and the ability to connect ages. In this investigation, we will dig into the meaning of children's songs, the significance of recording and sharing them, the job of innovation, and the manners by which this training can save social legacy, cultivate association, and praise the general insight of life as a parent.

1. **The Meaning of Bedtime songs**

1. **All inclusiveness of Bedtime songs**
   Bedtime songs are a social consistent, rising above topographical, phonetic, and fleeting limits. They have been sung to babies for centuries, offering comfort and warmth in each edge of the globe. Regardless of etymological and local contrasts, the major motivation behind bedtime songs continues as before: to give solace, love, and a feeling that everything is good to kids.

2. **Holding and Profound Association**
   Cradlesongs hold a remarkable spot in the parent-youngster relationship. The demonstration of singing a cradlesong can fortify the close to home connection between a parental figure and a newborn child. The delicate, melodic tones give solace, confirming the kid's trust and security in their parental figure.

3. **Social Legacy**
   Cradlesongs are melodies as well as vessels of social legacy. They convey the narratives, values, and customs of a general public. The songs, verses, and the demonstration of singing cradlesongs are passed down from one age to another, safeguarding the quintessence of a culture.

4. **Mental Advantages**

Research has shown that bedtime songs have mental advantages for the two newborn children and guardians. They can diminish pressure and tension, manage the child's pulse, and advance sound rest designs. Moreover, singing children's songs can give close to home help and unwinding to guardians.

II. Recording Bedtime songs: Saving Social Legacy

1. **The Significance of Documentation**
   In a quickly impacting world, customs and social practices are frequently in danger of being lost. Recording bedtime songs is a method for documentation, guaranteeing that these significant social components are protected for people in the future.

2. **Language Conservation**

   Cradlesongs are in many cases sung in local dialects, and as dialects advance and become imperiled, children's songs can act as semantic time containers. Recording them can add to language conservation endeavors and support the proceeded with utilization of these dialects.

3. **Oral Practice**

   Cradlesongs are in many cases passed down orally starting with one age then onto the next. Recording them helps protect the songs as well as the subtleties of articulation, mood, and profound articulation that might be lost over the long haul.

4. **Documenting and Computerized Vaults**

Present day innovation has made it more straightforward to record, file, and offer bedtime songs. Advanced stores, sound accounts, and on-line stages can act as significant assets for future examination and social safeguarding.

III. Innovation and Cradlesong Safeguarding

1. **Sound Recording**

   With the appearance of reasonable and versatile sound recording innovation, catching children's songs has become more open than any time in recent memory. Cell phones, compact sound recorders, and even voice-recording applications make it simple for parental figures to record their children's songs.

2. **Video Recording**

   Video recording catches the hear-able part of bedtime songs as well as the visual articulations and non-verbal communication of parental figures and youngsters. It adds one more layer of social extravagance to the safeguarding system.

3. **Online Stages and Computerized Vaults**

   The web offers a stage for imparting children's songs to a worldwide crowd. Different sites and web-based entertainment stages empower individuals to transfer and share their cradlesongs, adding to a tremendous computerized chronicle of these social pearls.

4. **Cooperative Endeavors**

Associations and analysts overall are dealing with projects that empower the recording and sharing of bedtime songs. Cooperative endeavors work with the assortment and dispersal of cradlesongs from different societies, making a worldwide embroidery of calming songs.

IV. The Force of Shared Children's songs

1. **Cultivating Association**
   Shared cradlesongs can be a scaffold among societies and ages. The demonstration of standing by listening to bedtime songs from various regions of the planet can make a feeling of association, sympathy, and understanding.

2. **Worldwide Point of view**
   Paying attention to children's songs from different societies gives a worldwide viewpoint and permits people to see the value in the variety and extravagance of human customs.

3. **Advancing Social Trade**
   Recording and sharing bedtime songs can advance social trade and exchange. The interaction can start discussions and interest in various social practices, stories, and values.

4. **Bringing issues to light**

As children's songs become more available through advanced stages, the world turns out to be progressively mindful of their worth as social fortunes. This mindfulness can prompt more noteworthy endeavors to save and praise these practices.

V. Difficulties and Contemplations

1. **Protection and Assent**
   Recording children's songs, particularly in a computerized age, brings up issues about security and assent. It is vital for regard the desires and inclinations of parental figures and networks while recording and sharing children's songs.
2. **Genuineness and Social Apportionment**
   While sharing cradlesongs from various societies, it is critical to do so deferentially and really. Keeping away from social apportionment and guaranteeing the appropriate setting is kept up with is fundamental.
3. **Moral Contemplations**
   While sharing children's songs, moral contemplations should direct the interaction. It is vital to consider the social and authentic settings and expected influences on the networks in question.
4. **Innovative Access**

Regardless of the advances in innovation, not all networks have equivalent admittance to recording and sharing stages. Endeavors ought to be made to connect the computerized partition and guarantee inclusivity.

11.4 The Impact of Arctic Aria on Conservation

The Cold, with its stunning scenes, one of a kind biological systems, and basic significance notwithstanding environmental change, is at the very front of worldwide ecological worries. While logical examination, strategy endeavors, and global joint efforts assume an essential part in Icy protection, creative articulations, for example, music have likewise demonstrated to be amazing assets in bringing issues to light and pushing for natural conservation. Icy Aria, a subgenre of music propelled by the Cold district, has turned into a medium through which performers, writers, and naturalists convey the excellence, delicacy, and desperation of rationing the Icy. In this broad investigation, we will dig into the meaning of the Icy Aria type, its part in preservation endeavors, its possible effect on approach, and the manners by which music can join individuals overall to safeguard the Cold.

1. **Cold Aria: A One of a kind Melodic Classification**
1. **Characterizing Cold Aria**
   Cold Aria is a classification of music that draws motivation from the Icy district, its scenes, societies, and the more extensive topic of natural protection. It frequently includes vocal exhibitions, traditional instrumentation, and electronic components, making a particular and suggestive sound that reflects the Cold's magnificence and secret.
2. **Beginnings and Advancement**
   The foundations of Cold Aria can be followed back to native Icy societies, where customary tunes have been sung for ages. Over the long run, contemporary writers and artists have embraced the class, consolidating current components and topics of natural promotion.
3. **Eminent Specialists and Authors**

A few craftsmen and writers have made critical commitments to Icy Aria. Figures like Eivør Pálsdóttir, Paul Winter, and Ludovico Einaudi have made organizations enlivened by the Cold, frequently determined to bring issues to light about environmental change and protection.

II. The Meaning of Cold Aria in Protection

1. **Bringing issues to light**
   Cold Aria fills in as an integral asset for bringing issues to light about the basic condition of the Icy. Its unpleasant tunes and suggestive verses make a close to home association, empowering individuals to look further into the area and its natural difficulties.
2. **Moving Points of view**
   Music can move a change in context. Icy Aria urges audience members to see the Cold as something beyond a far off, distant

district however as a crucial piece of our interconnected world that requests insurance and regard.

3. Profound Effect

The profound effect of music can't be undervalued. Icy Aria evokes a feeling of wonderment, compassion, and obligation in its audience members, driving them to draw in with Cold preservation endeavors on a more profound level.

III. The Job of Icy Aria in Natural Backing

1. **Joint efforts with Natural Associations**
   Specialists and arrangers who make Icy Aria frequently work together with ecological associations. These organizations assist with raising assets, support logical exploration, and work with protection drives in the Cold.

2. **Shows and Exhibitions**
   Icy Aria is frequently exhibited through live exhibitions, giving a stage to convey the desperation of Icy protection. Such occasions draw in a different crowd and consider a more unique interaction to the reason.

3. **Instructive Drives**
   Icy Aria is utilized in instructive projects to draw in understudies and the more extensive public in Icy preservation. Music turns into a showing device, assisting people with better comprehension the district's environment and the dangers it faces.

4. **Promotion through Media**

The openness of music through different media channels, including streaming stages and web-based entertainment, permits Cold Aria to contact a worldwide crowd and supporter for Icy protection on an uncommon scale.

IV. The Effect of Icy Aria on Strategy

1. **Forming General Assessment**

   By bringing issues to light and cultivating a more profound association with the Cold, Icy Aria can possibly impact popular assessment and request political activity. It can make a groundswell of help for Icy preservation.

2. **Political Promotion**

   Artists and writers who are enthusiastic about the Cold can become advocates for strategy change. They utilize their foundation to draw in with government officials, empower strategy conversations, and call for protection measures.

3. **Effect on Peaceful accords**

The force of music rises above borders. Cold Aria can possibly motivate global participation and impact arrangements that plan to safeguard the Icy's delicate biological systems and native societies.

V. The Potential for Social Trade

1. **Spanning Partitions**

   Cold Aria has the ability to connect splits among Icy and non-Icy countries, between mainstream researchers and the overall population, and between native societies and the more extensive world. A general language rises above etymological and social hindrances.

2. **Encouraging Compassion**

   Standing by listening to Cold Aria can cultivate compassion by permitting individuals to associate with the accounts and encounters of those living in the Icy. It empowers grasping, regard, and a common feeling of obligation.

3. **Observing Variety**

Cold Aria praises the social variety of the Icy, displaying the rich practices and legacy of native people groups and featuring the significance of saving these remarkable societies.

VI. Difficulties and Contemplations

1. Social Apportionment

At the point when non-native craftsmen draw in with Icy Aria, there is a gamble of social allotment. It is fundamental for specialists to move toward the class with deference, coordinated effort, and social responsiveness.

2. Offsetting Imaginative Articulation with Protection Informing

Specialists should track down a harmony between imaginative articulation and conveying a protection message. The music should stay bona fide while successfully conveying the criticalness of Cold preservation.

3. Estimating Effect

Assessing the effect of Cold Aria on preservation endeavors can challenge. While plainly the class brings issues to light, estimating substantial results as far as strategy change and preservation progress is a complicated errand.